Printed in Great Britain
by Amazon.co.uk, Ltd.,
Marston Gate.

Siddur
Tehillot HaMashiach

Praises of the Messiah

Linear • Hebrew & English
Transliterated

Erev Shabbat • Shabbat Morning Service
Additional Blessings

TorahResource • 2008

Softcover Edition
©2008 TorahResource
All Rights Reserved
ISBN 13: 978-0-9889581-8-0

Available from www.torahresource.com

Unless otherwise noted, Scripture quotations are from the
New American Standard Bible Update
Copyright © 1960, 1962, 1963, 1968, 1971, 1972,
1973, 1975, 1977, 1995 by The Lockman Foundation
All rights reserved

1 2 3 4 5 6 7 8 9 10

Table of Contents

Preface 4
Transliteration chart 5
Erev Shabbat in the Home
    Lighting Candles 7
    Psalms 9
    Blessing the Wife (*Eshet Chayil*) 17
    Blessing the Husband 20
    Blessing Single Adults 22
    Blessing Children 23
    Kiddush for Shabbat 24
    Hand Washing 26
    Blessing for the Challah (*HaMotzi*) 26
    Songs (*Z'mirot*) 27
    Blessing After the Meal (*Birkat HaMazon*) 29
Shabbat Morning Service
    Blessings for putting on a tallit / *Ma Tovu* 47
    Barchu 48
    Shema 51
    Sh'monei Esrei (Amidah) 60
    Messianic Confessions 74
    Torah Service 77
    Blessings before & after reading Torah 82
    Blessing before reading Haftarah 84
    Blessing before reading Apostolic Scriptures 85
    Blessing after reading Haftarah & Apostolic Scriptures 85
    Ashrei 90
    Half Kaddish 93
    Aleinu (Alternative) 94
    Aleinu (Traditional) 95
    Mourner's Kaddish 97
    Aaronic Benediction 99
    Blessing for Rosh Chodesh (New Month) 99
Havdalah 101
Prayer When Retiring at Night 105
Circumcision Service 117
Marriage Service 122
Prayers & Blessings 126

Preface

Luke gives us a notice about the early followers of Yeshua (Acts 2:42): "They were continually devoting themselves to the apostles' teaching and to fellowship, to the breaking of bread and to prayer." What the English translation leaves out is the word "the" which should be inserted before "prayer"– they were continually devoting themselves to "the prayer." They were devoting themselves to the teaching of the Apostles, no doubt centered around the manner in which the Tanach foretold the coming of Yeshua, His death and resurrection, and the victory He would win for all who would receive Him. They also maintained a fervent fellowship which included eating together. But perhaps one of the most vital components in their newly formed community was expressing their faith through the well-known prayers of the Synagogue.

I think praying liturgical prayers has great benefit, but it requires *kavvanah* — concentration. Like anything, these ancient prayers, blessings, and meditations can grow common if one does not set his or her heart and mind to worship the Almighty by confessing His greatness and His grace. I hope the pages that follow will afford some material for deep reflection upon the God we serve.

The text of his siddur is traditional (generally following nusach Ashkenaz) and I have departed from tradition only where it was deemed necessary to align with a biblically sound Messianic faith. I have put the name Yeshua in some places where it seems obvious to me it belongs. The English translations are my own, but of course, there are only so many alternatives in translating a standard text, so my translation is often very close to the many other traditional siddurim that contain English translations. At times, the translation is constrained by the linear format. The translation of the Scriptures is most often the NASB. In some cases I have given my own translation. The Hebrew transliteration follows Sephardic pronunciation.

My greatest hope is that these traditional prayers will be as much blessing to you as they have been and are to me and my family. May HaShem's blessing be upon us and upon all Israel as we seek Him.

Tim Hegg, Director
TorahResource

Tranliteration of Hebrew

Phonetic Sound	English	Hebrew
silent	none	א
b v	b = with dagesh v = no dagesh	בּ / ב
hard g as in go	g	ג
d	d	ד
h (silent at end of word)	h	ה
v	v	ו
z	z	ז
ch as in Bach	ch	ח
t	t	ט
y as in yellow	y	י
k ch as in Bach	k = with dagesh ch = no dagesh	כּ / ך
l	l	ל
m	m	מ / ם
n	n	נ / ן
s	s	ס
silent	none	ע
p f	p = with dagesh f = no dagesh	פּ / פ / ף
like ts in cats	tz	צ / ץ
q	q	ק
r	r	ר
s	s	שׂ
sh	sh	שׁ

In the transliteration, I have aimed at helping the non-Hebrew reader to pronounce the words correctly. Of course, any transliteration scheme is going to be only partially successful. Accentuation becomes a major issue. Generally, Hebrew tends to throw the accent to the end of the word. Exceptions often include those words with double seghol (e.g., 'emet) or double patach (e.g., tachat), in which case the accent shifts to the opening syllable. I have separated syllables in the transliteration with dashes in hopes that this will aid pronunciation.

Transliteration of Vowels

The Hebrew vowels are transliterated according to the following scheme:

אָ/אַ	"a" as in "father" (e.g., אָב = *av*)
אָ or אֳ	(*chametz chatuf*) - "o" as in "home" (e.g., אֳנִיָּה = *oniyah*)
אִ or אִי	"i" as in "machine" (e.g., הִיא = *hi* pronounced "hee")
אֵ	sometimes "e" as in "get" (e.g., כֵּן = *ken*) but sometimes "ei" as in "weigh" (e.g., יֵלֵךְ = *yei-leich*)
אֵי	"ei" as in "weigh" (e.g., בֵּית = *beit*)
אֶ	"e" as in "get" (e.g., חֶסֶד = *chesed*)
אֶי	either "e" as "get" or "ei" as in "weigh"
אֹ or אוֹ	"o" as in "home" (e.g., הוֹלֵךְ = *ho-leich*)
אֻ or אוּ	"u" as in "ruby" (e.g., בָּרוּךְ = *ba-ruch*)
אְ	when vocal, transliteratied by ' – quick, short "e" as in "petunia" (e.g., שְׁמַע = *sh'-ma*)
אַי or אָי	"ai" as in "aisle" (e.g., אֱלֹהַיִךְ = *Elohaich*)

Transliteration of the *sheva:* The pronunciation of the *vocal sheva* has been a point of contention throughout the history of the Hebrew Language. I have followed the grammatical scheme that considers every *sheva* as vocal when it follows a long vowel, whenever it is the opening vowel of a syllable, and when it is preceded by *meteg* in the Masoretic text. I have usually marked vocal *sheva* with a superscript dash e.g. תְּ.

Use of Large Type: In the Shabbat Morning Service, the first word or phrase of a section is put in Large Type (Hebrew) or **bold** (English) to indicate that the congregation joins the *chazzan* in reciting that particular part of the liturgy. The congregant is therefore alerted to those sections which require that they join the *chazzan* in vocal prayer. Of course, each *chazzan* should feel free to direct congregational participation according to their own liturgical tradition.

The Divine Name

The Divine Name, יהוה, is regularly translated by the accepted "Adonai" (and occasionally "HaShem"). When the Divine Name יָהּ, *Yah,* is encountered, and where the context warrants it, it is translated "Yah." The common term "Halleluyah" is generally left in this conventional form, but where the context warrants, may be translated "Praise Yah."

Welcoming the Sabbath
להדליק נרות Lighting Candles

The woman of the house (or any adult woman present) acts out the part of Moses who received the Torah on Mt. Sinai. She covers her head even as Moses was covered with a veil when he descended the mountain. After lighting the candles, she encircles them with her hands, drawing (as it were) the light to her eyes. This symbolizes Moses' request to see God's glory. Then she covers her eyes with her hands, again symbolizing God's response to Moses' request, that one cannot see the face of God and live. She then recites the blessing:

Traditional Blessing for Lighting Sabbath Candles

בָּרוּךְ אַתָּה יהוה Blessed are You, Adonai
Baruch ata Adonai

אֱלֹהֵינוּ מֶלֶךְ הָעוֹלָם our God, King of the Universe
Eloheinu melech ha-olam

אֲשֶׁר קִדְּשָׁנוּ Who sanctified us
asher kid'-shanu

בְּמִצְוֹתָיו with His commandments
b'mitz-vo-tav

וְצִוָּנוּ לְהַדְלִיק and commanded us to kindle
v'-tzi-vanu l'-had-lik

נֵר שֶׁל שַׁבָּת the lights of Sabbath
ner shel shabbat

Since the lighting of Sabbath Candles is a tradition and not commanded in the written Torah, an alternative blessing has been included here, emphasizing the biblical command to sanctify the Sabbath.

Alternative Blessing for Lighting Sabbath Candles

בָּרוּךְ אַתָּה יהוה Blessed are You, Adonai
Baruch ata Adonai

אֱלֹהֵינוּ מֶלֶךְ הָעוֹלָם our God, King of the Universe
Eloheinu melech ha-olam

אֲשֶׁר קִדְּשָׁנוּ Who sanctified us
asher kid'-shanu

בְּמִצְוֹתָיו with His commandments
b'mitz-vo-tav

וְצִוָּנוּ לְקַדֵּשׁ and commanded us to sanctify
v'-tzi-vanu l'-ka-deish

אֶת יוֹם הַשַּׁבָּת the Sabbath day.
et yom ha-shabbat

Erev Shabbat

שלום עליכם Shalom Aleichem

A traditional Sabbath song, welcoming the angels of the Most High to attend our Sabbath celebration, to bring peace to us and our household, and to enjoy the shalom of Sabbath with us.

שָׁלוֹם עֲלֵיכֶם Peace be upon you,
shalom a-lei-chem
מַלְאֲכֵי הַשָּׁרֵת ministering messengers,
mal-a-chei ha-sha-ret
מַלְאֲכֵי עֶלְיוֹן messengers of the Most High
mal-a-chei el-yon
מִמֶּלֶךְ מַלְכֵי הַמְּלָכִים from the King, the King of kings
mi-melech mal-chei ha-m'-la-chim
הַקָּדוֹשׁ בָּרוּךְ הוּא the Holy One, blessed be He!
ha-ka-dosh ba-ruch hu

בּוֹאֲכֶם לְשָׁלוֹם May you come to peace.
bo-a-chem l'-shalom
מַלְאֲכֵי הַשָּׁלוֹם messengers of peace,
mal-a-chei ha-shalom
מַלְאֲכֵי עֶלְיוֹן messengers of the Most High
mal-a-chei el-yon
מִמֶּלֶךְ מַלְכֵי הַמְּלָכִים from the King, the King of kings
mi-melech mal-chei ha-m'-la-chim
הַקָּדוֹשׁ בָּרוּךְ הוּא the Holy One, blessed be He!
ha-ka-dosh ba-ruch hu

בָּרְכוּנִי לְשָׁלוֹם Bless us with peace,
bar-chu-ni l'-shalom
מַלְאֲכֵי הַשָּׁלוֹם messengers of peace,
mal-a-chei ha-shalom
מַלְאֲכֵי עֶלְיוֹן messengers of the Most High
mal-a-chei el-yon
מִמֶּלֶךְ מַלְכֵי הַמְּלָכִים from the King, the King of kings
mi-melech mal-chei ha-m'-la-chim
הַקָּדוֹשׁ בָּרוּךְ הוּא the Holy One, blessed be He!
ha-ka-dosh ba-ruch hu

צֵאתְכֶם לְשָׁלוֹם Depart in peace,
tzei-t'-chem l'-shalom
מַלְאֲכֵי הַשָּׁלוֹם messengers of peace,
mal-a-chei ha-sha-lom
מַלְאֲכֵי עֶלְיוֹן messengers of the Most High,
mal-a-chei el-yon
מִמֶּלֶךְ מַלְכֵי הַמְּלָכִים from the King, the King of kings
mi-melech mal-chei ha-m'-la-chim
הַקָּדוֹשׁ בָּרוּךְ הוּא the Holy One, blessed be He!
ha-ka-dosh ba-ruch hu

Psalm 92

מִזְמוֹר שִׁיר לְיוֹם הַשַּׁבָּת	A Psalm, a Song for the Sabbath day	miz-mor shir l'yom ha-shabbat
טוֹב לְהֹדוֹת לַיהוה	It is good to give thanks to Adonai	tov l'-ho-dot la-Adonai
וּלְזַמֵּר לְשִׁמְךָ	And to sing praises to Your Name	u-l'-za-meir l'-shim-cha
עֶלְיוֹן לְהַגִּיד	O Most High; To declare	El-yon l'-ha-gid
בַּבֹּקֶר חַסְדֶּךָ	Your lovingkindness in the morning,	ba-boker chas-decha
וֶאֱמוּנָתְךָ בַּלֵּילוֹת	And Your faithfulness by night.	ve-e-mu-na-t'-cha ba-lei-lot
עֲלֵי־עָשׂוֹר	With the ten-stringed lute	a-lei a-sor
וַעֲלֵי־נָבֶל	and with the harp;	va-a-lei na-vel
עֲלֵי הִגָּיוֹן בְּכִנּוֹר	With resounding music upon the lyre.	a-lei hi-ga-yon b'-chi-nor
כִּי שִׂמַּחְתַּנִי יהוה	For You, Adonai, have made me glad	ki si-mach-ta-ni Adonai
בְּפָעֳלֶךָ	by what You have done;	b'-fa-o-lecha
בְּמַעֲשֵׂי יָדֶיךָ	at the works of Your hands	b'-ma-a-sei ya-de-cha
אֲרַנֵּן	I will sing for joy!	a-ra-nein
מַה־גָּדְלוּ מַעֲשֶׂיךָ יהוה	How great are Your works, Adonai!	ma ga-d'-lu ma-a-secha Adonai
מְאֹד עָמְקוּ מַחְשְׁבֹתֶיךָ	Your thoughts are very deep.	m'-od a-m'-ku mach-sh'-vo-techa
אִישׁ־בַּעַר לֹא יֵדָע	A senseless man has no knowledge	ish ba-ar lo yei-da
וּכְסִיל לֹא־יָבִין אֶת־זֹאת	Nor does a stupid man understand this,	u-ch'-sil lo ya-vin et zot
בִּפְרֹחַ רְשָׁעִים	That when the wicked sprouted up	bif-ro-ach r'-sha-im
כְּמוֹ עֵשֶׂב	like grass,	k'-mo ei-sev
וַיָּצִיצוּ כָּל־פֹּעֲלֵי אָוֶן	And all who did iniquity flourished,	va-ya-tzi-zu kol po-a-lei a-ven
לְהִשָּׁמְדָם	It was only that they might be destroyed	l'-hi-sha-m'-dam
עֲדֵי־עַד	forevermore.	a-dei ad

Erev Shabbat

וְאַתָּה מָרוֹם לְעֹלָם יהוה — But You, Adonai, are on high forever.
v'-atah ma-rom l'-olam Adonai

כִּי הִנֵּה אֹיְבֶיךָ יהוה — For, behold, Your enemies, Adonai;
ki hi-nei o-y'-vecha Adonai

כִּי־הִנֵּה אֹיְבֶיךָ יֹאבֵדוּ — For, behold, Your enemies will perish.
ki hi-nei o-y'-vecha yo-vei-du

יִתְפָּרְדוּ כָּל־פֹּעֲלֵי אָוֶן — All who do iniquity will be scattered.
yit-pa-r'-du kol po-a-lei a-ven

וַתָּרֶם — But You have exalted
va-ta-rem

כִּרְאֵים קַרְנִי — my horn like that of the wild ox;
kir-eim kar-ni

בַּלֹּתִי בְּשֶׁמֶן רַעֲנָן — I have been anointed with fresh oil
ba-lo-ti b'-shemen ra-a-nan

וַתַּבֵּט עֵינִי — And my eye has looked exultantly
va-ta-beit ei-ni

בְּשׁוּרָי — upon my foes.
b'-shu-rai

בַּקָּמִים עָלַי מְרֵעִים — When evil ones raise up against me
ba-ka-mim a-lai m'-rai-im

תִּשְׁמַעְנָה אָזְנָי — my ears hear of it.
tish-ma-na oz-nai

צַדִּיק — The righteous man
tza-dik

כַּתָּמָר יִפְרָח — will flourish like the palm tree,
ka-ta-mar yif-rach

כְּאֶרֶז בַּלְּבָנוֹן יִשְׂגֶּה — He will grow like a cedar in Lebanon,
k'-erez ba-l'-va-non yis-geh

שְׁתוּלִים בְּבֵית יהוה — Planted in the house of Adonai,
sh'-tu-lim b'-veit Adonai

בְּחַצְרוֹת אֱלֹהֵינוּ — In the courts of our God
b'-chatz-rot Eloheinu

יַפְרִיחוּ — They will flourish.
yaf-ri-chu

עוֹד יְנוּבוּן בְּשֵׂיבָה — They will still yield fruit in old age;
od y'-nu-vun b'-sei-vah

דְּשֵׁנִים וְרַעֲנַנִּים יִהְיוּ — They will be full of sap and very green
d'-shei-nim v'-ra-a-na-nim yi-h'-yu

לְהַגִּיד כִּי־יָשָׁר יהוה — To declare that Adonai is upright.
l'-ha-gid ki ya-shar Adonai

צוּרִי — He is my rock
tzu-ri

וְלֹא־עַוְלָתָה בּוֹ — and there is no unrighteousness in Him.
v'-lo o-la-tah bo

10

Psalm 95

Erev Shabbat

לְכוּ נְרַנְּנָה לַיהוה O come, let us sing for joy to Adonai,
l'-chu n'ra-n'-nah la-Adonai

נָרִיעָה לְצוּר Let us shout joyfully to the rock
na-ri-ah l'-tzur

יִשְׁעֵנוּ of our salvation.
yish-ei-nu

נְקַדְּמָה פָנָיו Let us come before Him
n'-ka-d'-mah fa-naiv

בְּתוֹדָה with thanksgiving,
b'-todah

בִּזְמִרוֹת נָרִיעַ לוֹ Let us shout joyfully to Him with songs.
biz-mi-rot na-ri-a lo

כִּי אֵל גָּדוֹל יהוה For Adonai is a great God
ki El gadol Adonai

וּמֶלֶךְ גָּדוֹל And a great King
u-melech ga-dol

עַל־כָּל־אֱלֹהִים above all gods,
al kol elohim

אֲשֶׁר בְּיָדוֹ In whose hand are the
asher b'-ya-do

מֶחְקְרֵי־אָרֶץ וְתוֹעֲפוֹת depths of the earth, The peaks of the
mech-k'-rei a-retz v'-to-a-fot

הָרִים לוֹ mountains are His also.
ha-rim lo

אֲשֶׁר־לוֹ הַיָּם The sea is His,
asher lo ha-yam

וְהוּא עָשָׂהוּ for it was He who made it,
v'-hu a-sa-hu

וְיַבֶּשֶׁת יָדָיו יָצָרוּ And His hands formed the dry land.
v'-ya-veshet ya-daiv ya-tza-ru

בֹּאוּ נִשְׁתַּחֲוֶה וְנִכְרָעָה Come, let us worship and bow down,
bo-u nish-ta-cha-veh v'-nich-ra-ah

נִבְרְכָה לִפְנֵי־יהוה עֹשֵׂנוּ Let us kneel before Adonai our Maker.
niv-r'-chah lif-nei Adonai o-seinu

כִּי הוּא אֱלֹהֵינוּ For He is our God,
ki hu Eloheinu

וַאֲנַחְנוּ עַם מַרְעִיתוֹ And we are the people of His pasture
va-a-nachnu am mar-i-to

וְצֹאן יָדוֹ and the sheep of His hand.
v'-tzon ya-do

הַיּוֹם אִם־בְּקֹלוֹ תִשְׁמָעוּ Today, if you would hear His voice,
ha-yom im b'-kolo tish-ma-u

אַל־תַּקְשׁוּ לְבַבְכֶם Do not harden your hearts,
al tak-shu l'-vav-chem

כִּמְרִיבָה כְּיוֹם מַסָּה	as at Meribah, As in the day of Massah	
	kim-ri-vah k'-yom ma-sah	
בַּמִּדְבָּר	in the wilderness,	
	ba-mid-bar	
אֲשֶׁר נִסּוּנִי אֲבוֹתֵיכֶם	When your fathers tested Me,	
	asher ni-suni a-vo-tei-chem	
בְּחָנוּנִי	They tried Me,	
	b'-cha-nuni	
גַּם־רָאוּ פָעֳלִי	though they had seen My work.	
	gam ra-u fa-a-li	
אַרְבָּעִים שָׁנָה	For forty years	
	ar-ba-im sha-nah	
אָקוּט בְּדוֹר	I loathed that generation,	
	a-kut b'-dor	
וָאֹמַר עַם	And said they are a people	
	va-o-mar am	
תֹּעֵי לֵבָב הֵם	who err in their heart,	
	to-ei lei-vav hem	
וְהֵם לֹא־יָדְעוּ דְרָכָי	And they do not know My ways.	
	v'-hem lo ya-d'-u d'-ra-chai	
אֲשֶׁר־נִשְׁבַּעְתִּי בְאַפִּי	Therefore I swore in My anger,	
	asher nish-ba-ti v'-a-pi	
אִם־יְבֹאוּן	Truly they shall not enter	
	im y'-vo-un	
אֶל־מְנוּחָתִי	into My rest.	
	el m'-nu-cha-ti	

Psalm 121

שִׁיר לַמַּעֲלוֹת	A Song of Ascents.	
	shir la-ma-a-lot	
אֶשָּׂא עֵינַי	I will lift up my eyes	
	e-sa ei-nai	
אֶל־הֶהָרִים	to the mountains;	
	el he-ha-rim	
מֵאַיִן יָבֹא עֶזְרִי	From where shall my help come?	
	mei-a-yin ya-vo ez-ri	
עֶזְרִי מֵעִם יהוה	My help comes from Adonai,	
	ez-ri mei-im Adonai	
עֹשֵׂה שָׁמַיִם וָאָרֶץ	Who made heaven and earth.	
	o-seih sha-ma-im va-a-retz	
אַל־יִתֵּן לַמּוֹט רַגְלֶךָ	He will not allow your foot to slip;	
	al yi-tein la-mot rag-lecha	
אַל־יָנוּם שֹׁמְרֶךָ	He who keeps you will not slumber.	
	al ya-num shom-re-cha	

Erev Shabbat

הִנֵּה לֹא־יָנוּם	Behold, He will neither slumber	*hi-nei lo ya-num*
וְלֹא יִישָׁן	nor sleep,	*v'-lo yi-shan*
שׁוֹמֵר יִשְׂרָאֵל	He Who keeps Israel.	*sho-meir Yisrael*
יהוה שֹׁמְרֶךָ	Adonai is your keeper;	*Adonai sho-m'-recha*
יהוה צִלְּךָ	Adonai is your shade	*Adonai tzi-l'-cha*
עַל־יַד יְמִינֶךָ	on your right hand.	*al yad y'-mi-necha*
יוֹמָם הַשֶּׁמֶשׁ לֹא־יַכֶּכָּה	The sun will not smite you by day,	*yo-mam ha-shemesh lo ya-ke-kah*
וְיָרֵחַ בַּלָּיְלָה	Nor the moon by night.	*v'-ya-rei-ach ba-la-y'-lah*
יהוה יִשְׁמָרְךָ	Adonai will protect you	*Adonai yish-ma-r'-cha*
מִכָּל־רָע	from all evil;	*mi-kol ra*
יִשְׁמֹר אֶת־נַפְשֶׁךָ	He will keep your soul.	*yish-mor et naf-she-cha*
יהוה יִשְׁמָר־צֵאתְךָ	Adonai will guard your going out	*Adonai yish-mar tzei-t'-cha*
וּבוֹאֶךָ	and your coming in	*u-vo-echa*
מֵעַתָּה וְעַד־עוֹלָם	From this time forth and forever.	*mei-atah v'ad olam*

Psalm 122

שִׁיר הַמַּעֲלוֹת לְדָוִד	A Song of Ascents, of David.	*shir ha-ma-a-lot l'-Da-vid*
שָׂמַחְתִּי בְּאֹמְרִים לִי	I was glad when they said to me,	*sa-mach-ti b'-om-rim li*
בֵּית יהוה נֵלֵךְ	Let us go to the house of Adonai.	*beit Adonai nei-leich*
עֹמְדוֹת הָיוּ רַגְלֵינוּ בִּשְׁעָרַיִךְ	Our feet are standing in your gates,	*o-m'-dot ha-yu rag-leinu bish-a-ra-yich*
יְרוּשָׁלָםִ	O Jerusalem,	*Y'-ru-sha-la-im*
יְרוּשָׁלַםִ הַבְּנוּיָה כְּעִיר	Jerusalem, that is built as a city	*Y'-ru-sha-la-im ha-b'-nu-yah k'-ir*
שֶׁחֻבְּרָה־לָּהּ יַחְדָּו	that is compact together;	*she-chu-b'-rah lah yach-dav*

Erev Shabbat

שֶׁשָּׁם עָלוּ שְׁבָטִים	To which the tribes go up,	she-sham a-lu sh'-va-tim
שִׁבְטֵי־יָהּ	even the tribes of Yah	shiv-tei Yah
עֵדוּת לְיִשְׂרָאֵל	An ordinance for Israel	ei-dut l'-Yisrael
לְהֹדוֹת לְשֵׁם	To give thanks to the name	l'-ho-dot l'-shem
יהוה	of Adonai	Adonai
כִּי שָׁמָּה יָשְׁבוּ כִסְאוֹת	For there thrones were set	ki sha-mah ya-sh'-vu chis-ot
לְמִשְׁפָּט כִּסְאוֹת	for judgment, the thrones	l'-mish-pat kis-ot
לְבֵית דָּוִיד	of the house of David.	l'-veit Da-vid
שַׁאֲלוּ שְׁלוֹם יְרוּשָׁלָָם	Pray for the peace of Jerusalem:	sha-a-lu shalom Y'-ru-sha-la-im
יִשְׁלָיוּ אֹהֲבָיִךְ	May they prosper who love you.	yish-lai-u o-ha-va-yich
יְהִי־שָׁלוֹם בְּחֵילֵךְ	May peace be within your walls,	y'-hi shalom b'-chei-leich
שַׁלְוָה	And prosperity	shal-vah
בְּאַרְמְנוֹתָיִךְ	within your palaces.	b'-ar-m'-no-ta-yich
לְמַעַן אַחַי	For the sake of my brothers	l'-ma-an a-chai
וְרֵעָי אֲדַבְּרָה־נָּא	and my friends, I will now say,	v'-rei-ai a-da-b'-rah na
שָׁלוֹם בָּךְ	"May peace be within you."	shalom bach
לְמַעַן בֵּית־יהוה	For the sake of the house of Adonai	l'-ma-an beit Adonai
אֱלֹהֵינוּ אֲבַקְשָׁה טוֹב לָךְ	our God, I will seek your good.	Eloheinu a-vak-sha tov lach

Psalm 128

שִׁיר הַמַּעֲלוֹת	A Song of Ascents.	shir ha-ma-a-lot
אַשְׁרֵי כָּל־יְרֵא יהוה	How blessed are all who fear Adonai,	ash-rei kol y'-rei Adonai
הַהֹלֵךְ בִּדְרָכָיו	Who walk in His ways.	ha-ho-leich bid-ra-chaiv

יְגִיעַ כַּפֶּיךָ כִּי תֹאכֵל	When you eat of the fruit of your hands,	
	y'-gi-a ka-peicha ki to-cheil	
אַשְׁרֶיךָ	You will be happy	
	ash-reicha	
וְטוֹב לָךְ	and it will be well with you.	
	v'-tov lach	
אֶשְׁתְּךָ כְּגֶפֶן פֹּרִיָּה	Your wife shall be like a fruitful vine	
	esh-t'-cha k'-gefen po-ri-yah	
בְּיַרְכְּתֵי בֵיתֶךָ בָּנֶיךָ	Within your house, Your children	
	b'-yar-k'-tei vei-techa ba-neicha	
כִּשְׁתִלֵי זֵיתִים	like olive plants	
	kish-ti-lei zei-tim	
סָבִיב לְשֻׁלְחָנֶךָ	Around your table.	
	sa-viv l'-shul-cha-necha	
הִנֵּה כִי־כֵן יְבֹרַךְ גָּבֶר	Behold, thus shall the man be blessed	
	hi-nei chi chen y'-vo-rach ga-ver	
יְרֵא יהוה	Who fears Adonai.	
	y'-rei Adonai	
יְבָרֶכְךָ יהוה מִצִּיּוֹן	Adonai bless you from Zion,	
	y'-va-re-k'-cha Adonai mi-tzi-yon	
וּרְאֵה בְּטוּב	And may you see the prosperity	
	u-r'-ei b'-tuv	
יְרוּשָׁלָיִם כֹּל יְמֵי חַיֶּיךָ	of Jerusalem all the days of your life.	
	Y'-ru-sha-la-im kol y'-mei cha-yeicha	
וּרְאֵה־	Indeed, may you see	
	u-r'-ei	
בָנִים לְבָנֶיךָ	your children's children.	
	va-nim l'-va-neicha	
שָׁלוֹם עַל־יִשְׂרָאֵל	Peace be upon Israel!	
	shalom al Yis-ra-el	

Psalm 146

הַלְלוּ־יָהּ	Hallelujah!	
	ha-l'-lu-Yah	
הַלְלִי נַפְשִׁי אֶת־יהוה	Praise Adonai, O my soul!	
	ha-l'-li naf-shi et Adonai	
אֲהַלְלָה יהוה בְּחַיָּי	I will praise Adonai while I live;	
	a-hal-lah Adonai b'-cha-ya	
אֲזַמְּרָה לֵאלֹהַי	I will sing praises to my God	
	a-za-m'-rah lei-lo-hai	
בְּעוֹדִי	while I have my being.	
	b'-o-di	
אַל־תִּבְטְחוּ בִנְדִיבִים	Do not trust in princes,	
	al tiv-t'-chu vin-di-vim	

Erev Shabbat

בְּבֶן־אָדָם	In mortal man,
	b'-ven a-dam
שֶׁאֵין לוֹ תְשׁוּעָה	in whom there is no salvation.
	she-ein lo t'-shu-ah
תֵּצֵא רוּחוֹ יָשֻׁב	His spirit departs, he returns
	tei-tzei ru-cho ya-shuv
לְאַדְמָתוֹ בַּיּוֹם הַהוּא	to the earth; In that very day
	l'-ad-ma-to ba-yom ha-hu
אָבְדוּ עֶשְׁתֹּנֹתָיו	his thoughts perish.
	a-v'-du esh-to-no-taiv
אַשְׁרֵי	How blessed is he
	ash-rei
שֶׁאֵל יַעֲקֹב בְּעֶזְרוֹ	whose help is the God of Jacob,
	she-Eil Ya-a-kov b'-ez-ro siv-ro
שִׂבְרוֹ עַל־יהוה אֱלֹהָיו	Whose hope is in Adonai his God,
	al Adonai E-lo-haiv
עֹשֶׂה שָׁמַיִם וָאָרֶץ	Who made heaven and earth,
	o-seh sha-ma-im va-a-retz
אֶת־הַיָּם וְאֶת־כָּל־אֲשֶׁר־בָּם	The sea and all that is in them;
	et ha-yam v'-et kol asher bam
הַשֹּׁמֵר אֱמֶת לְעוֹלָם	Who keeps truth forever;
	ha-sho-meir emet l'-olam
עֹשֶׂה מִשְׁפָּט	Who executes justice
	o-seh mish-pat
לָעֲשׁוּקִים נֹתֵן לֶחֶם	for the oppressed; Who gives food
	la-a-shu-kim no-tein lechem
לָרְעֵבִים	to the hungry.
	la-r'-ei-vim
יהוה מַתִּיר אֲסוּרִים	Adonai sets the prisoners free.
	Adonai ma-tir a-su-rim
יהוה פֹּקֵחַ עִוְרִים	Adonai opens the eyes of the blind;
	Adonai po-chei-ach iv-rim
יהוה זֹקֵף	Adonai raises up
	Adonai zo-keif
כְּפוּפִים	those who are bowed down;
	k'-fu-fim
יהוה אֹהֵב צַדִּיקִים	Adonai loves the righteous;
	Adonai o-heiv tza-di-kim
יהוה שֹׁמֵר אֶת־גֵּרִים	Adonai protects the strangers;
	Adonai sho-meir et gei-rim
יָתוֹם וְאַלְמָנָה	The fatherless and the widow,
	ya-tom v'-al-ma-nah
יְעוֹדֵד וְדֶרֶךְ	He supports; But the way
	y'-o-deid v'-derech

רְשָׁעִים יְעַוֵּת of the wicked He thwarts.
r'-sha-im y'-a-veit
יִמְלֹךְ יהוה לְעוֹלָם Adonai will reign forever,
yim-loch Adonai l'-olam
אֱלֹהַיִךְ צִיּוֹן Your God, O Zion,
E-lo-ha-yich Tzi-yon
לְדֹר וָדֹר הַלְלוּ־יָהּ to all generations. Halleluyah!
l'-dor va-dor ha-l'-lu-Yah

Blessings Upon the Family

It is a beautiful tradition to extend blessings to family members at the Erev Shabbat table. Included here are blessings for the wife (said by the husband), the husband (said by the wife) and for the children (said by either father or mother). Also included is an additional blessing for single adults who may be part of the Shabbat celebration. Since Shabbat is a foretaste of eternity when God's blessings upon His people will be eternally manifest, our desire to bless each other is a foreshadow of the world to come.

Blessing upon the Wife (Proverbs 31:10-31)

אֵשֶׁת־חַיִל מִי יִמְצָא An excellent wife, who can find?
eishet cha-yil mi yim-tza
וְרָחֹק מִפְּנִינִים מִכְרָהּ For her worth is far above jewels.
v'-ra-chok mi-p'-ni-nim mich-rah
בָּטַח בָּהּ לֵב בַּעְלָהּ The heart of her husband trusts in her,
ba-tach bah leiv ba-'e-lah
וְשָׁלָל לֹא יֶחְסָר And he will have no lack of gain.
v'-sha-lal lo yech-sar
גְּמָלַתְהוּ טוֹב וְלֹא־רָע She does him good and not evil
g'-ma-lat-hu tov v'-lo ra
כֹּל יְמֵי חַיֶּיהָ All the days of her life.
kol i'-mei cha-yei-ha
דָּרְשָׁה צֶמֶר וּפִשְׁתִּים She looks for wool and flax
da-r'-shah tzemer u-fish-tim
וַתַּעַשׂ בְּחֵפֶץ כַּפֶּיהָ And works with her hands in delight.
va-ta-as b'-chei-fetz ka-pei-ha
הָיְתָה כָּאֳנִיּוֹת She is like merchant ships;
ha-y'-tah ka-o-ni-yot
סוֹחֵר מִמֶּרְחָק תָּבִיא From afar she brings
so-cheir mi-mer-chok ta-vim
לַחְמָהּ her food.
lach-mah
וַתָּקָם בְּעוֹד לַיְלָה She rises also while it is still night
va-ta-kam b'-ot la-y'-lah

Erev Shabbat

וַתִּתֵּן טֶרֶף לְבֵיתָהּ	And gives food to her household	
	va-ti-tein teref l'-vei-tah	
וְחֹק לְנַעֲרֹתֶיהָ	And portions to her maidens.	
	v'-chok l'-na-a-ro-tei-ha	
זָמְמָה שָׂדֶה וַתִּקָּחֵהוּ	She considers a field and buys it;	
	za-m'-mah sa-deh va-ti-ka-chei-hu	
מִפְּרִי כַפֶּיהָ נָטְעָה כָּרֶם	From her earnings she plants a vineyard.	
	mi-p'-ri cha-pei-ha na-t'-ah ka-rem	
חָגְרָה בְעוֹז מָתְנֶיהָ	She girds herself with strength	
	cha-g'-rah v'-oz ma-t'-nei-ha	
וַתְּאַמֵּץ זְרוֹעוֹתֶיהָ	And makes her arms strong.	
	va-t'-a-meitz z'-ro-o-tei-ha	
טָעֲמָה כִּי־טוֹב סַחְרָהּ	She senses that her gain is good;	
	ta-a-mah ki-tov sach-rah	
לֹא־יִכְבֶּה בַלַּיְלָה נֵרָהּ	Her lamp does not go out at night.	
	lo yich-veh va-la-y'-lah nei-rah	
יָדֶיהָ שִׁלְּחָה בַכִּישׁוֹר	She puts her hand to the distaff,	
	ya-dei-ha shi-l'-chah va-ki-shor	
וְכַפֶּיהָ תָּמְכוּ פָלֶךְ	And her hands grasp the spindle.	
	v'-cha-pei-ha ta-m'-chu fa-lech	
כַּפָּהּ פָּרְשָׂה לֶעָנִי	She extends her hand to the poor,	
	ka-hah pa-r'-sah le-o-ni	
וְיָדֶיהָ שִׁלְּחָה	And she stretches out her hands	
	v'-ya-dei-ha shi-l'-chah	
לָאֶבְיוֹן	to the needy.	
	la-ev-yon	
לֹא־תִירָא	She is not afraid	
	lo ti-ra	
לְבֵיתָהּ מִשָּׁלֶג	of the snow for her household,	
	l'-vei-tah mi-sha-leg	
כִּי כָל־בֵּיתָהּ	For all her household are	
	ki chol bei-tah	
לָבֻשׁ שָׁנִים	clothed with scarlet.	
	la-vush sha-nim	
מַרְבַדִּים עָשְׂתָה־לָּהּ	She makes coverings for herself;	
	mar-va-dim a-s'-tah lah	
שֵׁשׁ וְאַרְגָּמָן	fine linen and purple	
	seish v'-ar-ga-man	
לְבוּשָׁהּ	are her clothing.	
	l'-vu-shah	
נוֹדָע בַּשְּׁעָרִים בַּעְלָהּ	Her husband is known in the gates,	
	no-da ba-sh'-a-rim ba-lah	
בְּשִׁבְתּוֹ עִם־	When he sits among	
	b'-shiv-to im	

Erev Shabbat

זִקְנֵי־אָרֶץ the elders of the land.
zik-nei a-retz

סָדִין עָשְׂתָה She makes linen garments
sa-din a-s'-tah

וַתִּמְכֹּר וַחֲגוֹר נָתְנָה and sells them, And supplies belts
va-tim-kor va-cha-gor na-t'-nah

לַכְּנַעֲנִי to the tradesmen.
la-k'-na-ani

עֹז־וְהָדָר לְבוּשָׁהּ Strength and dignity are her clothing,
oz v'-ha-dar l'-vu-shah

וַתִּשְׂחַק לְיוֹם אַחֲרוֹן And she smiles at the future.
va-tis-chak l'-yom a-cha-ron

פִּיהָ פָּתְחָה בְחָכְמָה She opens her mouth in wisdom,
pi-ha pa-t'-chah v'-cha-ch'-mah

וְתוֹרַת־חֶסֶד And the teaching of kindness is
v'-to-rat chesed

עַל־לְשׁוֹנָהּ on her tongue.
al l'-sho-nah

צוֹפִיָּה הֲלִיכוֹת She looks well to the ways
tzo-fi-yah ha-li-chot

בֵּיתָהּ of her household,
bei-tah

וְלֶחֶם עַצְלוּת And the bread of idleness
v'-lechem atz-lut

לֹא תֹאכֵל she does not eat.
lo to-cheil

קָמוּ בָנֶיהָ וַיְאַשְּׁרוּהָ Her children rise up and bless her;
ka-mu va-ne-yah va-y'-a-sh'-ru-ha

בַּעְלָהּ וַיְהַלְלָהּ Her husband also, and he praises her:
ba-'e-lah va-y'-hal-lah

רַבּוֹת בָּנוֹת עָשׂוּ חָיִל "Many daughters have done nobly,
ra-bot ba-not a-su cha-yil

וְאַתְּ עָלִית עַל־כֻּלָּנָה But you excel them all."
v'-at a-lit al ku-la-nah

שֶׁקֶר הַחֵן וְהֶבֶל הַיֹּפִי Charm is deceitful and beauty is fleeting,
she-ker ha-chen v'-hevel ha-yo-fi

אִשָּׁה יִרְאַת־יהוה But a woman who fears Adonai,
i-sha yir-at Adonai

הִיא תִתְהַלָּל she shall be praised.
hi tit-ha-lal

תְּנוּ־לָהּ מִפְּרִי יָדֶיהָ Give her the fruit of her hands, and
t'-nu lah mi-p'-ri ya-de-yah

וִיהַלְלוּהָ בַשְּׁעָרִים מַעֲשֶׂיהָ Let her works praise her in the gates.
vi-hal-lu-ha va-sh'-a-rim ma-a-se-ha

Erev Shabbat

Blessing upon the Husband

In modern times, it has become traditional for the wife also to say a blessing over her husband. Two Psalms have been included to choose from, or one could select another portion of Scripture for the blessing.

Psalm 1

אַשְׁרֵי־הָאִישׁ אֲשֶׁר לֹא Blessed is the man who does not
ash-rei ha-ish asher lo

הָלַךְ בַּעֲצַת רְשָׁעִים walk in the counsel of the wicked,
halach ba-a-tzat r'-sha-im

וּבְדֶרֶךְ חַטָּאִים לֹא עָמָד nor stand in the way of sinners,
u-v'-derech cha-ta-im lo a-mad

וּבְמוֹשַׁב לֵצִים לֹא יָשָׁב nor sit in the seat of scoffers;
u-v'-mo-shav lei-tzim lo ya-shav

כִּי אִם בְּתוֹרַת יהוה חֶפְצוֹ For his delight is in the Torah of Adonai
ki im b'-to-rat Adonai chef-tzo

וּבְתוֹרָתוֹ יֶהְגֶּה and in His Torah he meditates
u-v'-to-ra-to yeh-geh

יוֹמָם וָלָיְלָה day and night.
yo-mam va-la-y'-lah

וְהָיָה כְּעֵץ שָׁתוּל He will be like a firmly planted tree
v'-ha-yah k'-eitz sha-tul

עַל־פַּלְגֵי מָיִם beside streams of water
al pal-gei ma-yim

אֲשֶׁר פִּרְיוֹ יִתֵּן בְּעִתּוֹ that gives its fruit in its season
asher pir-yo yi-tein b'-i-to

וְעָלֵהוּ לֹא־יִבּוֹל and its leaf does not wither;
v'-a-lei-hu lo yi-bol

וְכֹל אֲשֶׁר־יַעֲשֶׂה יַצְלִיחַ and in all that he does, he prospers.
v'-chol asher ya-a-seh yatz-li-ach

לֹא־כֵן הָרְשָׁעִים The wicked are not so,
lo chen ha-r'-sha-im

כִּי אִם־כַּמֹּץ אֲשֶׁר־ but are like chaff which is
ki im ka-motz asher

תִּדְּפֶנּוּ רוּחַ blown by the wind.
ti-d'-fe-nu ru-ach

עַל־כֵּן לֹא־יָקֻמוּ רְשָׁעִים Therefore the wicked will not stand
al ken lo ya-ku-mu r'-sha-im

בַּמִּשְׁפָּט וְחַטָּאִים in judgment nor sinners
ba-mish-pat v'-cha-ta-im

בַּעֲדַת צַדִּיקִים in the congregation of the righteous;
ba-a-dat tza-di-kim

כִּי־יוֹדֵעַ יהוה For Adonai knows
ki yo-dei-a Adonai

דֶּרֶךְ צַדִּיקִים the way of the righteous,
derech tza-di-kim

וְדֶרֶךְ רְשָׁעִים תֹּאבֵד but the way of the wicked will perish
v'-derech r'-sha-im to-veid

Psalm 112

הַלְלוּ יָהּ HalleluYah!
ha-l'-lu Yah

אַשְׁרֵי־אִישׁ יָרֵא אֶת־יהוה Blessed is the man who fears Adonai,
ash-rei ish ya-rei et Adonai

בְּמִצְוֹתָיו חָפֵץ מְאֹד Who greatly delights in His mitzvot.
b'-mitz-vo-taiv cha-feitz m'-od

גִּבּוֹר בָּאָרֶץ יִהְיֶה זַרְעוֹ His seed will be mighty on the earth;
gi-bor ba-a-retz yih-yeh zar-o

דּוֹר יְשָׁרִים The generation of the upright
dor y'-sha-rim

יְבֹרָךְ will be blessed.
y'-vo-rach

הוֹן־וָעֹשֶׁר בְּבֵיתוֹ Wealth and riches are in his house,
hon va-o-sher b'-vei-to

וְצִדְקָתוֹ עֹמֶדֶת לָעַד And his righteousness endures forever.
v'-tzid-ka-to o-medet la-ad

זָרַח בַּחֹשֶׁךְ אוֹר Light arises in the darkness
za-rach ba-cho-shech or

לַיְשָׁרִים for the upright;
la-y'-sha-rim

חַנּוּן וְרַחוּם He is gracious and compassionate
cha-nun v'-ra-chum

וְצַדִּיק and righteous.
v'-tza-dik

טוֹב־אִישׁ חוֹנֵן It is well with the man who is gracious
tov ish cho-nein

וּמַלְוֶה and lends;
u-mal-veh

יְכַלְכֵּל דְּבָרָיו בְּמִשְׁפָּט He will maintain his cause in judgment.
y'-chal-cheil d'-va-raiv b'-mish-pat

כִּי־לְעוֹלָם לֹא־יִמּוֹט For he will never be shaken;
ki l'-o-lam lo yi-mot

לְזֵכֶר עוֹלָם יִהְיֶה צַדִּיק The righteous will be remembered forever.
l'-zei-cher o-lam yih-yeh tza-dik

מִשְּׁמוּעָה רָעָה לֹא יִירָא He will not fear evil tidings;
mi-sh'-mu-ah ra-ah lo yi-ra

נָכוֹן לִבּוֹ His heart is steadfast,
na-chon li-bo

Erev Shabbat

בָּטֻחַ בַּיהוה trusting in Adonai
ba-tu-ach ba-Adonai

סָמוּךְ לִבּוֹ לֹא יִירָא His heart is upheld, he will not fear,
sa-much li-bo lo yi-ra

עַד אֲשֶׁר־יִרְאֶה Until he looks
ad asher yir-eh

בְצָרָיו פִזַּר with satisfaction on his adversaries.
b'-tza-raiv pi-zar

נָתַן לָאֶבְיוֹנִים He has given freely to the poor,
na-tan la-ev-yo-nim

צִדְקָתוֹ עֹמֶדֶת לָעַד His righteousness endures forever;
tzid-ka-to o-medet la-ad

קַרְנוֹ תָּרוּם בְּכָבוֹד His horn will be exalted in honor.
kar-no ta-rum b'-cha-vod

רָשָׁע יִרְאֶה וְכָעָס The wicked will see it and be vexed,
ra-sha yir-eh v'-cha-as

שִׁנָּיו יַחֲרֹק He will gnash his teeth
shi-naiv ya-cha-rok

וְנָמָס and melt away;
v'-na-mas

תַּאֲוַת רְשָׁעִים תֹּאבֵד The desire of the wicked will perish.
ta-a-vat r'-sha-im to-veid.

Blessing for Single Adults

When single adults are present at the Erev Shabbat table, the host may desire to give the following blessing on their behalf:

Psalm 84:4, 5, 11, 12 [Hebrew 84:5, 6, 12, 13]

אַשְׁרֵי יוֹשְׁבֵי How blessed are those who dwell
ashrei yo-sh'-vei

בֵיתֶךָ in Your House,
vei-te-cha

עוֹד יְהַלְלוּךָ סֶּלָה continually praising You. (selah)
od y'-ha-l'-lu-cha (se-lah)

אַשְׁרֵי אָדָם How blessed is the person
ashrei adam

עוֹז־לוֹ בָךְ whose strength is in You;
oz lo vach

מְסִלּוֹת בִּלְבָבָם the highways *to Zion* are in their heart.
m'-si-lot bil-va-vam

כִּי שֶׁמֶשׁ וּמָגֵן יהוה אֱלֹהִים For Adonai God is a sun and shield
ki shemesh u-ma-gein Adonai Elohim

Erev Shabbat

חֵן וְכָבוֹד יִתֵּן יהוה Adonai gives grace and honor
chein v'-cha-vod yi-tein Adonai
לֹא יִמְנַע־טוֹב No good thing will He withhold
lo yim-na tov
לַהֹלְכִים בְּתָמִים from those who walk uprightly.
la-ho-l'-chim b'-ta-mim
יהוה צְבָאוֹת Adonai of Hosts—
Adonai tz'-va-ot
אַשְׁרֵי אָדָם How blessed is the person
ashrei adam
בֹּטֵחַ בָּךְ who trusts in You!
bo-tei-ach bach

Blessing over the Children

The traditional blessings are said by the Father or Mother over the young children at the table, fulfilling the prophecy of Genesis 48:20. The traditional blessings incorporate the hope that the children will one day establish their own families where the worship of Israel's God will continue. The parents may want to add their own personal prayer of blessing as well.

Blessing over Sons

יְשִׂמְךָ אֱלֹהִים May God establish you
y'-sim-cha Elohim
כְּאֶפְרַיִם וְכִמְנַשֶּׁה like Ephraim and Manasseh[1]
k'-ef-ra-im v'-chim-na-shah

Blessing over Daughters

יְשִׂמֵךְ אֱלֹהִים May God establish you
y'-si-mach Elohim
כְּשָׂרָה רִבְקָה רָחֵל וְלֵאָה like Sarah, Rebecca, Rachel, and Leah
k'-sa-rah riv-kah ra-cheil v'-lei-ah

(1) Gen 48:20

Erev Shabbat

Final Blessing over All (the Priestly Blessing)
Numbers 6:22-24

Since the destruction of the Temple and the loss of the priesthood, it has become the tradition for the head of the house (or any adult) to pronounce the Priestly Blessing over all who are at the Shabbat Table

יְבָרֶכְךָ יהוה וְיִשְׁמְרֶךָ Adonai bless you and keep you;
y'-va-re-ch'-cha Adonai v'-yish-m'-recha

יָאֵר יהוה פָּנָיו Adonai cause His face to shine
ya-eir Adonai pa-naiv

אֵלֶיךָ וִיחֻנֶּךָּ upon you and be gracious to you;
ei-lecha vi-chu-ne-cha

יִשָּׂא יהוה פָּנָיו אֵלֶיךָ Adonai lift up His face toward you
yi-sa Adonai pa-naiv ei-lecha

וְיָשֵׂם לְךָ שָׁלוֹם and grant you His shalom.
v'-ya-seim l'-cha shalom

Shabbat Kiddush

The Kiddush (sanctification) incorporates the fruit of the vine, a symbol of joy. We set apart (sanctify) the Sabbath as a day of joy and gladness to HaShem. Everyone should have wine or juice for the Kiddush, and in some traditions, everyone stands while reciting the Kiddush.

Genesis 2:1-3

וַיְהִי עֶרֶב וַיְהִי בֹקֶר And there was evening and morning,
va-y'-hi erev va-ya-hi vo-ker

יוֹם הַשִּׁשִּׁי וַיְכֻלּוּ הַשָּׁמַיִם the sixth day. Completed were the heavens
yom ha-shi-shi va-y'-chu-lu ha-sha-ma-im

וְהָאָרֶץ וְכָל־צְבָאָם and the earth, and all their host.
v'-ha-a-retz v'-chol tz'-va-am

וַיְכַל אֱלֹהִים And God finished,
va-y'-chal Elohim

בַּיּוֹם הַשְּׁבִיעִי מְלַאכְתּוֹ on the seventh day, His work
ba-yom ha-sh'-vi-i m'-la-ch'-to

אֲשֶׁר עָשָׂה וַיִּשְׁבֹּת which He had done; and He ceased
asher a-sah va-yish-bot

בַּיּוֹם הַשְּׁבִיעִי on the seventh day
ba-yom ha-sh'-vi-i

מִכָּל־מְלַאכְתּוֹ אֲשֶׁר עָשָׂה from all His work which He had done.
mi-kol m'-la-ch'-to asher a-sah

וַיְבָרֶךְ אֱלֹהִים And God blessed
va-y'-va-rech Elohim

אֶת־יוֹם הַשְּׁבִיעִי וַיְקַדֵּשׁ the seventh day and sanctified
et yom ha-sh'-vi-i va-y'-ka-deish

אֹתוֹ כִּי בוֹ שָׁבַת it because on it He ceased
oto ki vo sha-vat

Erev Shabbat

מִכָּל־מְלַאכְתּוֹ אֲשֶׁר־בָּרָא from all His work of creating
mi-kol m'-la-ch'-to asher ba-ra
אֱלֹהִים לַעֲשׂוֹת which God had done.
Elohim la-a-sot

Everyone joins in for the blessing over the wine:

בָּרוּךְ אַתָּה יהוה אֱלֹהֵינוּ Blessed are You, Adonai our God
baruch ata Adonai Eloheinu
מֶלֶךְ הָעוֹלָם King of the Universe,
melech ha-o-lam
בּוֹרֵא פְּרִי הַגָּפֶן Creator of the fruit of the vine.
bo-rei p'-ri ha-ga-fen

בָּרוּךְ אַתָּה יהוה אֱלֹהֵינוּ Blessed are You, Adonai our God
baruch ata Adonai Eloheinu
מֶלֶךְ הָעוֹלָם King of the Universe,
melech ha-o-lam
אֲשֶׁר קִדְּשָׁנוּ בְּמִצְוֹתָיו Who sanctified us with His mitzvot
asher ki-d'-sha-nu b'-mitz-vo-taiv
וְרָצָה בָנוּ and took pleasure in us,
v'-ra-tzah va-nu
וְשַׁבַּת קָדְשׁוֹ בְּאַהֲבָה and His holy Sabbath, in love
v'-sha-bat ko-d'-sho b'-a-ha-vah
וּבְרָצוֹן הִנְחִילָנוּ and in pleasure, He has bequeathed to us,
u-v'-ra-tzon hin-chi-lanu
זִכָּרוֹן לְמַעֲשֵׂה בְרֵאשִׁית a memorial of the creation,
zi-ka-ron l'-ma-a-seih v'-rei-shit
כִּי הוּא יוֹם תְּחִלָּה a day which is the beginning of
ki hu yom t'-chi-lah
לְמִקְרָאֵי קֹדֶשׁ our sacred gatherings,
l'-mik-ra-ei ko-desh
זֵכֶר לִיצִיאַת מִצְרָיִם a memorial of our exodus from Egypt.
zei-cher li-tzi-at mitz-ra-im
כִּי בָנוּ בָחַרְתָּ For You chose us,
ki vanu va-char-ta
וְאוֹתָנוּ קִדַּשְׁתָּ מִכָּל הָעַמִּים and sanctified us from all the peoples
v'-o-tanu ki-dash-ta mi-kol ha-a-mim
וְשַׁבַּת קָדְשְׁךָ בְּאַהֲבָה and Your holy Sabbath, in love
v'-sha-bat kod-sh'-cha b'-a-ha-vah
וּבְרָצוֹן הִנְחַלְתָּנוּ and in pleasure, You bequeathed to us.
u-v'-ra-tzon hin-chal-ta-nu
בָּרוּךְ אַתָּה יהוה Blessed are You Adonai
baruch ata Adonai
מְקַדֵּשׁ הַשַּׁבָּת Sanctifier of the Sabbath.
m'-ka-deish ha-sha-bat

Erev Shabbat

Washing Hands (נְטִילַת יָדָיִם)

As we anticipate sharing the meal together, we recognize that it symbolizes the covenant of which we are all members. Washing hands is a symbolic reminder that as members together in Yeshua's congregation, we are to have lives that are made clean by His sanctifying work through the Spirit.

James 4:8
Draw near to God and He will draw near to you. Cleanse your hands, you sinners; and purify your hearts, you double-minded.

Psalm 24:3–4
Who may ascend into the hill of Adonai? And who may stand in His holy place? He who has clean hands and a pure heart, Who has not lifted up his soul to falsehood and has not sworn deceitfully.

It is traditional to have the children help pass a basin and pitcher, and to carry the towel so that each person at the table can wash their hands. In their acting as servants, they model Yeshua Himself Who washed the disciples' feet. The blessing is said and then hands are washed:

בָּרוּךְ אַתָּה יהוה   Blessed are You, Adonai
baruch ata Adonai
אֱלֹהֵינוּ מֶלֶךְ הָעוֹלָם   our God, King of the Universe,
Eloheinu melech ha-o-lam
אֲשֶׁר קִדְּשָׁנוּ בְּמִצְוֹתָיו   Who sanctified us with His mitzvot
asher ki-d'-sha-nu b'-mitz-vo-taiv
וְצִוָּנוּ עַל נְטִילַת יָדָיִם   and commanded us about washing hands.
v'-tzi-vanu al n'-ti-lat ya-da-im

Blessing for the Challah (המוציא)

The Challah (Sabbath bread) symbolizes the sacrifices in the Temple, and is thus a reminder of the sacrifice of Messiah for us. Two loaves represent the morning and evening sacrifices; they also remind us that we were to gather twice as much manna on the sixth day in order to rest on the Sabbath. The Challah, woven together, reminds us of the mystery of the incarnation; it is sweet, reflects the light of the candles, and is broken for all to partake. Salt is added to the first bite to remind us of the salt which was added to sacrifices in the Temple.

בָּרוּךְ אַתָּה יהוה   Blessed are You, Adonai
baruch ata Adonai
אֱלֹהֵינוּ מֶלֶךְ הָעוֹלָם   our God, King of the Universe,
Eloheinu melech ha-o-lam
הַמּוֹצִיא לֶחֶם מִן הָאָרֶץ   Who brings forth bread from the earth.
ha-mo-tzi le-chem min ha-aretz

Erev Shabbat

Z'mirot זמירות (Songs)

1. Yom Zeh L'Yisrael

יוֹם זֶה לְיִשְׂרָאֵל — This is a day for Israel
yom zeh l'-Yisrael

אוֹרָה וְשִׂמְחָה — of light and joy;
orah v'-simchah

שַׁבָּת מְנוּחָה — a Shabbat of rest.
shabbat m'-nu-chah

2. Hinei Mah Tov

הִנֵּה מַה טּוֹב — Behold how good
hinei mah tov

וּמַה נָּעִים — and how pleasant it is
u-mah na-im

שֶׁבֶת אַחִים — for brethren to dwell together
shevet achim

גַּם יָחַד — in unity.
gam ya-chad

3. Yedid Nefesh

יְדִיד נֶפֶשׁ — Lover of my soul;
yedid nefesh

אָב הָרַחֲמָן — Father of compassion
av ha-ra-cha-man

מְשׁוֹךְ עַבְדְּךָ אֶל רְצוֹנְךָ — Draw your servant to Your will
m'-shoch av-d'-cha el r'-tzo-n'-cha

יָרוּץ עַבְדְּךָ כְּמוֹ אַיָּל — Your servant will run like a deer;
ya-rutz av-d'-cha k'-mo a-yal

יִשְׁתַּחֲוֶה אֶל מוּל הֲדָרֶךָ — He will bow before Your glory.
yish-ta-cha-v'h el mul ha-da-re-cha

Yedid nefesh av ha-rachaman
Lover of my soul, Draw me to Your will!
Ya-rutz av-de-cha ke-mo a-yal
As a deer runs to her home
Master I run to Your throne

Erev Shabbat

4. Hinei El Yeshuati (Isaiah 12:2)

הִנֵּה אֵל יְשׁוּעָתִי
Behold God is my salvation;
hinei El y'-shu-a-ti

אֶבְטַח וְלֹא אֶפְחָד
I will trust and not be afraid
ev-tach v'-lo ef-chad

כִּי־עָזִּי וְזִמְרָת יָהּ יהוה
For Yah Adonai is my strength and song
ki a-zi v'-zim-rat Yah HaShem

וַיְהִי־לִי לִישׁוּעָה
He also has become my salvation!
va-y'-hi li li-shu-ah

5. Esa Einai (Psalm 121:1-2)

אֶשָּׂא עֵינַי אֶל־הֶהָרִים
I lift my eyes to the hills;
e-sa einai el he-ha-rim

מֵאַיִן יָבֹא עֶזְרִי
Where will my help come from?
mei-a-yin ya-vo ez-ri

עֶזְרִי מֵעִם יהוה
My help *comes* from Adonai
ez-ri mei-im HaShem

עֹשֵׂה שָׁמַיִם וָאָרֶץ
Maker of heaven and earth!
o-sei sha-ma-im va-aretz

6. Lo Ya-reiu (Isaiah 11:9)

לֹא־יָרֵעוּ וְלֹא־יַשְׁחִיתוּ
They will not hurt or destroy
lo ya-rei-u v'-lo yash-chi-tu

בְּכָל־הַר קָדְשִׁי
in all My holy mountain.
b'-chol har kod-shi

כִּי־מָלְאָה הָאָרֶץ
For the earth will be full of
ki mal-ah ha-aretz

דֵּעָה אֶת־יהוה
the knowledge of Adonai
dei-ah et HaShem

כַּמַּיִם לַיָּם מְכַסִּים
As the waters cover the sea.
ka-ma-yim la-yam m'-cha-sim

7. HaShiveinu (Lam 5:21)

הֲשִׁיבֵנוּ יהוה אֵלֶיךָ
Cause us to return to You, Adonai
ha-shi-vei-nu HaShem ei-le-cha

וְנָשׁוּבָה
and we will return;
v'-na-shu-vah

חַדֵּשׁ יָמֵינוּ כְּקֶדֶם
Renew our days as of old!
cha-deish ya-mei-nu k'-kedem

ברכת המזון Birkat Hamazon

לשבת ויום טוב: תהלים קכו For Shabbat and Yom Tov: Psalm 126

שִׁיר הַמַּעֲלוֹת A Song for Ascending
shir ha-ma-a-lot

בְּשׁוּב יהוה אֶת שִׁיבַת When Adonai brought back the exiled
b'shuv Adonai et shi-vat

צִיּוֹן הָיִינוּ כְּחֹלְמִים: of Zion we were like dreamers.
Tzi-on ha-yinu k'-chol-mim.

אָז יִמָּלֵא שְׂחוֹק פִּינוּ Then our mouths were filled with laughter
az yi-ma-lei s'-chok pi-nu

וּלְשׁוֹנֵנוּ רִנָּה and our tongues with joyful song.
u-l'-sho-neinu ri-na

אָז יֹאמְרוּ בַגּוֹיִם Then they will say among the nations
az yo-m'-ru va-goy-im

הִגְדִּיל יהוה לַעֲשׂוֹת "Adonai has done great things
hig-dil Adonai la-a-sot

עִם אֵלֶּה: with them!"
im ei-leh.

הִגְדִּיל יהוה לַעֲשׂוֹת עִמָּנוּ Adonai has done great things with us:
Hig-dil Adonai la-asot i-manu

הָיִינוּ שְׂמֵחִים: We were rejoicing.
ha-yinu s'-mei-chim

שׁוּבָה יהוה אֶת שְׁבִיתֵנוּ Adonai, return our exiles
shu-vah Adonai et sh'-vi-tei-nu

כַּאֲפִיקִים בַּנֶּגֶב: like the streams in the Negev.
ka-a-fi-kim ba-negev

הַזֹּרְעִים בְּדִמְעָה Those who sow in tears,
ha-zor-im b'-dim-ah

בְּרִנָּה יִקְצֹרוּ: with joyous song will they reap.
b'-rinah yik-tzo-ru

הָלוֹךְ יֵלֵךְ וּבָכֹה Though he goes out and weeps,
ha-loch yei-leich u-va-cho

נֹשֵׂא מֶשֶׁךְ הַזָּרַע carrying the bag of seed—
no-sei me-shech ha-za-ra

בֹּא יָבֹא בְרִנָּה Surely he will come with a joyous song,
bo ya-vo v'-ri-nah

נֹשֵׂא אֲלֻמֹּתָיו: bearing his sheaves of grain.
no-sei a-lu-mo-taiv

Birchat HaMazon

*On weekdays Psalm 137 is recited
in memory of the destruction of the Temple*

עַל נַהֲרוֹת בָּבֶל
By the rivers of Babylon
al na-ha-rot Ba-vel

שָׁם יָשַׁבְנוּ גַּם בָּכִינוּ
there we sat and wept,
sham ya-shavnu gam ba-chinu

בְּזָכְרֵנוּ אֶת צִיּוֹן:
when we remembered Zion.
b'-zach-reinu et Tzi-yon.

עַל עֲרָבִים בְּתוֹכָהּ
Upon the willows in her midst
al a-ra-vim b'-to-chah

תָּלִינוּ כִּנֹּרוֹתֵינוּ:
we hung our harps.
ta-linu ki-no-ro-teinu.

כִּי שָׁם שְׁאֵלוּנוּ
For there our captors asked of us
ki sham sh'-ei-lu-nu sho-veinu

שׁוֹבֵינוּ דִּבְרֵי שִׁיר
words of song,
div-rei shir

וְתוֹלָלֵינוּ שִׂמְחָה
and our tormentors asked for rejoicing.
v'-to-la-leinu simchah

שִׁירוּ לָנוּ מִשִּׁיר צִיּוֹן:
"Sing for us from the songs of Zion!"
shiru lanu mi-shir Tzi-yon

אֵיךְ נָשִׁיר אֶת שִׁיר
How can we sing the song of
eich na-shir et shir

יהוה עַל אַדְמַת נֵכָר:
Adonai on foreign soil?
Adonai al ad-mat nei-char.

אִם אֶשְׁכָּחֵךְ יְרוּשָׁלָיִם
If I forget you, Jerusalem,
im esh-ka-cheich Y'ru-sha-la-yim

תִּשְׁכַּח יְמִינִי:
may my right hand forget *its skill.*
tish-kach y'-mi-ni.

תִּדְבַּק לְשׁוֹנִי לְחִכִּי
May my tongue cleave to my palate,
tid-bak l'-shoni l'-chi-ki

אִם לֹא אֶזְכְּרֵכִי
If I fail to remember you,
im lo ez-k'-rei-chi

אִם לֹא אַעֲלֶה אֶת
if I fail to raise
im lo a-aleh et

יְרוּשָׁלַיִם עַל
Jerusalem above my
Y'ru-sh-la-yim al

רֹאשׁ שִׂמְחָתִי:
highest joy.
rosh sim-cha-ti.

זְכֹר יהוה לִבְנֵי
Remember, Adonai, against the sons of
z'-chor Adonai liv-nei

אֱדוֹם אֵת יוֹם יְרוּשָׁלָיִם
Edom, the day of Jerusalem.
E-dom et yom Y'ru-sha-la-yim

הָאֹמְרִים
For they were saying
ha-o-m'-rim

Birchat HaMazon

עָרוּ עָרוּ עַד הַיְסוֹד בָּהּ: "Raze it, raze it to the foundation!"
aru aru ad ha-y'-sod bah.

בַּת בָּבֶל Daughter of Babylon,
bat Bavel

הַשְּׁדוּדָה you are the devastated one!
ha-sh'-du-dah

אַשְׁרֵי שֶׁיְּשַׁלֶּם לָךְ Fortunate is he who will repay you
ash-rei she-y'-sha-lem lach

אֶת גְּמוּלֵךְ שֶׁגָּמַלְתְּ לָנוּ: for all you have done to us!
et g'mu-leich she-ga-malt lanu

אַשְׁרֵי שֶׁיֹּאחֵז וְנִפֵּץ Fortunate is he who will seize and dash
ash-rei she-yo-cheiz v'-ni-peitz

אֶת עֹלָלַיִךְ אֶל הַסָּלַע: your little ones on the rock!
et o-la-la-yich el ha-sa-la.

(One person should be designated as the Leader)

Leader begins:

רַבּוֹתַי נְבָרֵךְ: My colleagues, let us say the blessing
ra-bo-tai n'-va-reich

The others respond:

יְהִי שֵׁם יהוה מְבֹרָךְ May the Name of Adonai be blessed
y'-hi shem Adonai m'-vo-rach

מֵעַתָּה וְעַד עוֹלָם From now and forever.
mei-atah v'ad o-lam

Leader repeats:

יְהִי שֵׁם יהוה מְבֹרָךְ May the Name of Adonai be blessed
y'-hi shem Adonai m'-vo-rach

מֵעַתָּה וְעַד עוֹלָם From now and forever.
mei-atah v'ad o-lam

Leader continues:
(add "our God" if ten or more are present)

בִּרְשׁוּת With your permission
bir-shut

מָרָנָן וְרַבָּנָן וְרַבּוֹתַי our leaders and teachers
ma-ra-nan v'-ra-ba-nan v'-ra-bo-tai

נְבָרֵךְ (אֱלֹהֵינוּ) let us bless (our God)
n'va-reich (Eloheinu)

שֶׁאָכַלְנוּ מִשֶּׁלּוֹ of Whose food we have eaten.
she-a-chal-nu mi-she-lo.

Birchat HaMazon

The others respond:

בָּרוּךְ (אֱלֹהֵינוּ) — Blessed is (our God)
baruch (Eloheinu)
שֶׁאָכַלְנוּ מִשֶּׁלּוֹ — of Whose food we have eaten
she-a-chal-nu mi-she-lo
וּבְטוּבוֹ חָיִינוּ — and by His goodness we live.
u-v'-tu-vo cha-yi-nu

The Leader repeats:

בָּרוּךְ (אֱלֹהֵינוּ) — Blessed is (our God)
baruch (Eloheinu)
שֶׁאָכַלְנוּ מִשֶּׁלּוֹ — of Whose food we have eaten
she-a-chal-nu mi-she-lo
וּבְטוּבוֹ חָיִינוּ — and by His goodness we live.
u-v'-tu-vo cha-yi-nu

All respond: (some add this response only if there is a minyan)

בָּרוּךְ הוּא וּבָרוּךְ שְׁמוֹ: — Blessed is He and blessed is His Name.
Baruch hu u-va-ruch sh'-mo

All continue:

בָּרוּךְ אַתָּה יהוה אֱלֹהֵינוּ — Blessed are You, Adonai our God
Baruch ata Adonai Eloheinu
מֶלֶךְ הָעוֹלָם — King of the universe
melech ha-olam
הַזָּן אֶת הָעוֹלָם כֻּלּוֹ — Who nourishes the whole world
ha-zan et ha-olam ku-lo
בְּטוּבוֹ בְּחֵן — in His goodness, grace,
b'-tu-vo b'-chen
בְּחֶסֶד וּבְרַחֲמִים — lovingkindness, and mercy.
b'-chesed u-v'-ra-cha-mim
הוּא נוֹתֵן לֶחֶם לְכָל בָּשָׂר — He gives bread to all flesh
hu no-tein lechem l'-chol va-sar
כִּי לְעוֹלָם חַסְדּוֹ — for His lovingkindness is eternal.
ki l'-olam chas-do.
וּבְטוּבוֹ הַגָּדוֹל — And in His great goodness
u-v'-tu-vo ha-ga-dol
תָּמִיד לֹא חָסַר לָנוּ — never do we lack
ta-mid lo cha-sar lanu
וְאַל יֶחְסַר לָנוּ מָזוֹן — and never will we lack food
v'-al yech-sar la-nu ma-zon
לְעוֹלָם וָעֶד — forever,
l'-olam va-ed
בַּעֲבוּר שְׁמוֹ הַגָּדוֹל — for His name sake.
ba-a-vur she-mo ha-ga-dol

Birchat HaMazon

כִּי הוּא אֵל
ki hu El
Because He is God,

זָן וּמְפַרְנֵס לַכֹּל
zan u-m'-far-nes la-kol
the nourisher and maintainer of all,

וּמֵטִיב לַכֹּל
u-mei-tiv la-chol
and the One Who does good to all

וּמֵכִין מָזוֹן לְכֹל
u-mei-chin ma-zon l'-chol b'ri-yo-tav
and prepares nourishment for all

בְּרִיּוֹתָיו אֲשֶׁר בָּרָא.
asher ba-ra
of His creatures which He created.

בָּרוּךְ אַתָּה יהוה
Baruch ata Adonai,
Blessed are You, Adonai,

הַזָּן אֶת הַכֹּל:
ha-zan et ha-chol
Who nourishes all.

נוֹדֶה לְךָ יהוה אֱלֹהֵינוּ
no-deh l'-cha Adonai Eloheinu
We thank You, Adonai, our God

עַל שֶׁהִנְחַלְתָּ לַאֲבוֹתֵינוּ
al she-hin-chal-tah la-a-vo-teinu
for giving an inheritance to our fathers,

אֶרֶץ חֶמְדָּה טוֹבָה וּרְחָבָה
eretz chem-dah tovah u-r'-cha-vah
a desireable, good, and spacious Land

וְעַל שֶׁהוֹצֵאתָנוּ יהוה
v'-al she-ho-tzei-tanu Adonai
and for bringing us out, Adonai

אֱלֹהֵינוּ מֵאֶרֶץ מִצְרַיִם
Eloheinu mei-eretz Mitzra-im
our God, from the land of Egypt,

וּפְדִיתָנוּ מִבֵּית עֲבָדִים
u-f'-di-tanu mi-beit a-va-dim
redeeming us from the house of slavery,

וְעַל בְּרִיתְךָ
v'-al b'-ri-t'-cha
and for Your covenant

שֶׁחָתַמְתָּ בִּבְשָׂרֵנוּ
she-cha-tam-ta biv-sa-reinu
sealed in our flesh,

וְעַל תּוֹרָתְךָ שֶׁלִּמַּדְתָּנוּ
v'-al to-ra-t'-cha she-li-mad-ta-nu
and for Your Torah which You teach us,

וְעַל חֻקֶּיךָ
v'al chu-kei-cha
and for Your statutes

שֶׁהוֹדַעְתָּנוּ
she-ho-da-ta-nu
which You made known to us,

וְעַל חַיִּים חֵן וָחֶסֶד
v'-al cha-yim chen va-chesed
and for life, grace, and lovingkindness

שֶׁחוֹנַנְתָּנוּ
she-cho-nan-ta-nu
which You have granted to us

וְעַל אֲכִילַת מָזוֹן שָׁאַתָּה
v'-al a-chi-lat ma-zon sha-a-ta
and for the food with which You

זָן וּמְפַרְנֵס אוֹתָנוּ תָּמִיד
zan u-m'-far-neis o-tanu ta-mid
have always nourished and sustained us

Birchat HaMazon

בְּכָל יוֹם וּבְכָל עֵת	every day, and at all times	b'-chol yom u-v'-chol eit
וּבְכָל שָׁעָה:	and in every hour.	u-v'-chol sha-a

(On Hanukkah and Purim, add the blessings in the shaded block)

עַל הַנִּסִּים	[We thank You] for the miracles,	al ha-ni-sim
וְעַל הַפֻּרְקָן	the redemption,	v'-al ha-pur-kan
וְעַל הַגְּבוּרוֹת	the mighty deeds,	v'-al ha-g'-vu-rot
וְעַל הַתְּשׁוּעוֹת	deliverances,	v'-al ha-t'-shu-ot
וְעַל הַמִּלְחָמוֹת שֶׁעָשִׂיתָ	and the wars which You accomplished	v'-al ha-mil-cha-mot she-a-sita
לַאֲבוֹתֵינוּ בַּיָּמִים הָהֵם	for our fathers in those days	la-a-vo-teinu ba-ya-mim ha-hem
בַּזְּמַן הַזֶּה.	at this time.	ba-z'-man ha-zeh.

(On Hanukkah)

בִּימֵי מַתִּתְיָהוּ בֶּן יוֹחָנָן	In the days of Matityahu son of Yochanan	bi-mei ma-tit-yahu ben Yochanan
כֹּהֵן גָּדוֹל חַשְׁמוֹנָאִי	the High Priest, the Hasmonean	kohen gadol chash-mo-na-i
וּבָנָיו כְּשֶׁעָמְדָה מַלְכוּת	and his sons, when the evil kingdom	u-va-naiv k'-she-am-dah mal-chut
יָוָן הָרְשָׁעָה עַל עַמְּךָ	of Greece rose up against Your people	Ya-van ha-r'-sha-ah al a-m'-cha
יִשְׂרָאֵל לְהַשְׁכִּיחָם	Israel, to force them to forget	Yis-rael l'-hash-ki-cham
תּוֹרָתֶךָ וּלְהַעֲבִירָם	Your Torah and to turn away	to-ra-te-cha u-l'-ha-a-vi-ram
מֵחֻקֵּי רְצוֹנֶךָ	from the statutes of Your delight—	mei-chu-kei r'-tzo-ne-cha
וְאַתָּה בְּרַחֲמֶיךָ הָרַבִּים	You, in Your great mercy,	v'-ata b'-ra-cha-mei-cha ha-ra-bim
עָמַדְתָּ לָהֶם בְּעֵת	stood for them in the time	a-mad-ta la-hem b'-eit
צָרָתָם רַבְתָּ אֶת רִיבָם	of their distress; You defended their cause,	tza-ra-tam tav-ta et rivam
דַּנְתָּ אֶת דִּינָם	You judged their grievances,	dan-ta et di-nam
נָקַמְתָּ אֶת נִקְמָתָם	You avenged them.	na-kam-ta et nik-ma-tam

Birchat HaMazon

מָסַרְתָּ גִבּוֹרִים You delivered the mighty
ma-sar-ta gi-borim

בְּיַד חַלָּשִׁים וְרַבִּים into the hand of the weak, and the many
b'-yad cha-la-shim v'-rabim

בְּיַד מְעַטִּים וּטְמֵאִים into the hand of the few, the defiled
b'-yad m'-atim u-t'-mei-im

בְּיַד טְהוֹרִים into the hand of the undefiled,
b'-yad t'-ho-rim

וּרְשָׁעִים בְּיַד and the wicked into the hand of
u-r'-sha-im b'-yad

צַדִּיקִים the righteous;
tza-di-kim

וְזֵדִים בְּיַד and the insolent into the hand of
v'-zei-dim b'-yad

עוֹסְקֵי תוֹרָתֶךָ the diligent students of Your Torah.
o-s'-kei to-ra-techa

וּלְךָ עָשִׂיתָ And You made for Yourself
u-l'-cha a-si-ta

שֵׁם גָּדוֹל וְקָדוֹשׁ בְּעוֹלָמֶךָ a great and holy Name in Your world
shem gadol v'-kadosh b'-o-la-mecha

וּלְעַמְּךָ יִשְׂרָאֵל עָשִׂיתָ and for Your people Israel You made
u-l'-a-m'-cha Yisrael a-sita

תְּשׁוּעָה גְדוֹלָה וּפֻרְקָן a great deliverance and redemption
t'-shuah g'-dolah u-fur-kan

כְּהַיּוֹם הַזֶּה as it is today.
k'-ha-yom hazeh

וְאַחַר כֵּן בָּאוּ בָנֶיךָ Afterward Your sons came
v'-a-char ken ba-u va-necha

לִדְבִיר בֵּיתֶךָ to the Most Holy Place of Your House
lid-vir vei-techa

וּפִנּוּ אֶת הֵיכָלֶךָ and they cleansed your Temple
u-finu et hei-cha-lecha

וְטִהֲרוּ אֶת מִקְדָּשֶׁךָ and purified Your sanctuary
v'-ti-ha-ru et mik-da-shecha

וְהִדְלִיקוּ נֵרוֹת and kindled the lights
v'-hid-liku nei-rot

בְּחַצְרוֹת קָדְשֶׁךָ in the courtyards of Your Sanctuary.
b'-chatz-rot kad-shecha

וְקָבְעוּ שְׁמוֹנַת יְמֵי So they designated these eight days
v'-ka-v'-u sh'-mo-nat y'-mei

חֲנֻכָּה אֵלּוּ לְהוֹדוֹת וּלְהַלֵּל of Hanukkah to thank and praise
cha-nu-kah ei-lu l'-ho-dot u-l'-halel

לְשִׁמְךָ הַגָּדוֹל Your great Name.
l'-shim-cha ha-gadol

Birchat HaMazon

(On Purim)

בִּימֵי מָרְדְּכַי וְאֶסְתֵּר In the days of Mordechai and Esther
bi-mei Mor-d'-chai v'-Es-teir

בְּשׁוּשַׁן הַבִּירָה in Shushan the Capital
b'-Shushan ha-bi-rah

כְּשֶׁעָמַד עֲלֵיהֶם when he stood against us,
k'-she-a-mad a-lei-hem

הָמָן הָרָשָׁע that evil Haman,
Ha-man ha-ra-sha

בִּקֵשׁ לְהַשְׁמִיד לַהֲרֹג he sought to destory, to kill,
bi-kesh l'-hash-mid la-ha-rog

וּלְאַבֵּד אֶת כָּל הַיְּהוּדִים and to wipe out all the Jews,
u-l'-a-beid et kol ha-Y'-hu-dim

מִנַּעַר וְעַד זָקֵן טַף young and old, nursing babes
mi-na-ar v'-ad za-kein taf

וְנָשִׁים בְּיוֹם אֶחָד and women, in one day,
v'-na-shim b'-yom echad

בִּשְׁלוֹשָׁה עָשָׂר on the thirteenth day
bish-lo-shah a-sar

לְחֹדֶשׁ שְׁנֵים עָשָׂר of the twelfth month,
l'-chodesh sh'-neim a-sar

הוּא חֹדֶשׁ אֲדָר that is, the month of Adar,
hu chodesh A-dar

וּשְׁלָלָם לָבוֹז and their wealth to plunder.
u-sh'-la-lam la-voz

וְאַתָּה בְּרַחֲמֶיךָ הָרַבִּים Yet You, in Your abundant compassion
v'-ata b'-ra-cha-mecha ha-ra-bim

הֵפַרְתָּ אֶת עֲצָתוֹ annulled his counsel,
hei-far-ta et a-tza-to

וְקִלְקַלְתָּ אֶת מַחֲשַׁבְתּוֹ and frustrated his schemes,
v'-kil-kal-ta et ma-cha-shav-to

וַהֲשֵׁבוֹתָ לּוֹ גְּמוּלוֹ and You returned to him his evil plan
va-ha-shei-vota lo g'mu-lo

בְּרֹאשׁוֹ וְתָלוּ אוֹתוֹ upon his head, and they hung him
b'-ro-sho v'-ta-lo oto

וְאֶת בָּנָיו עַל הָעֵץ and his sons upon the wooden gallows.
v'-et ba-naiv al ha-eitz

וְעַל הַכֹּל יהוה אֱלֹהֵינוּ For everything, Adonai our God
v'-al ha-kol Adonai Eloheinu

אֲנַחְנוּ מוֹדִים לָךְ we thank You
a-nach-nu modim lach

וּמְבָרְכִים אוֹתָךְ and we bless You.
u-m'-var-chim o-tach

Birchat HaMazon

יִתְבָּרַךְ שִׁמְךָ בְּפִי Blessed is Your Name in the mouth
yit-barach shim-cha b'-fi

כָּל חַי תָּמִיד לְעוֹלָם וָעֶד of all the living, always, forever,
kol chai tamid l'-olam va-ed

כַּכָּתוּב as it is written:
ka-katuv

וְאָכַלְתָּ וְשָׂבָעְתָּ and you shall eat and be satisfied
v'-a-chal-ta v'-sa-va-ta

וּבֵרַכְתָּ אֶת יהוה אֱלֹהֶיךָ and you shall bless Adonai your God
u-vei-rach-ta et Adonai Eloheicha

עַל הָאָרֶץ הַטֹּבָה אֲשֶׁר נָתַן for the good Land which
al ha-a-retz ha-tovah asher

לָךְ:[1] He gave to you.[1]
na-tan lach

בָּרוּךְ אַתָּה יהוה Blessed are You, Adonai,
Baruch ata Adonai

עַל הָאָרֶץ וְעַל הַמָּזוֹן: for the Land and for the food.
al ha-aretz v'-al ha-ma-zon.

רַחֵם נָא יהוה אֱלֹהֵינוּ Please have compassion, Adonai our God,
rachem na Adonai Eloheinu

עַל יִשְׂרָאֵל עַמֶּךָ upon Israel Your people,
al Yisrael a-mecha

וְעַל יְרוּשָׁלַיִם עִירֶךָ upon Jerusalem Your city,
v'-al Y'-ru-sha-la-yim i-re-cha

וְעַל צִיּוֹן מִשְׁכַּן כְּבוֹדֶךָ upon Zion the place Your glory dwells,
v'-al Tzi-yon mish-kan k'-vo-decha

וְעַל מַלְכוּת בֵּית דָּוִד upon the kingdom of David's house
v'-al mal-chut beit Da-vid

מְשִׁיחֶךָ Your anointed,
m'-shi-che-cha

וְעַל הַבַּיִת הַגָּדוֹל וְהַקָּדוֹשׁ and upon the great and holy House
v'-al ha-ba-it ha-gadol v'-ha-ka-dosh

שֶׁנִּקְרָא שִׁמְךָ עָלָיו which is called by Your Name.
she-nik-ra shim-cha a-laiv

אֱלֹהֵינוּ אָבִינוּ רְעֵנוּ Our God, our Father, shepherd us,
Eloheinu a-vi-nu r'-ei-nu

זוּנֵנוּ פַּרְנְסֵנוּ nourish us, maintain us,
zu-nei-nu par-n'-sei-nu

וְכַלְכְּלֵנוּ וְהַרְוִיחֵנוּ sustain us, relieve us,
v'-chal-k'-lei-nu v'-har-vi-chei-nu

וְהַרְוַח לָנוּ יהוה אֱלֹהֵינוּ and grant us relief, Adonai our God,
v'-har-vach lanu Adonai Eloheinu

מְהֵרָה מִכָּל צָרוֹתֵינוּ quickly from all our troubles.
m'-hei-rah mi-kol tza-ro-tei-nu

(1) Deut 8:10

Birchat HaMazon

וְנָא אֶל תַּצְרִיכֵנוּ And please, may we not be in need
v'-na al tatz-ri-cheinu

יהוה אֱלֹהֵינוּ Adonai our God
Adonai Eloheinu

לֹא לִידֵי מַתְּנַת בָּשָׂר וָדָם not from the gifts of mankind,
lo li-dei ma-t'-nat ba-sar va-dam

וְלֹא לִידֵי הַלְוָאָתָם nor of their aid,
v'-lo li-dei hal-va-a-tam

כִּי אִם לְיָדְךָ הַמְּלֵאָה but only from Your hand which is full,
ki im l'-ya-d'-cha ha-m'-lei-a

הַפְּתוּחָה הַקְּדוֹשָׁה open, holy,
ha-p'-tu-cha ha-k'-do-shah

וְהָרְחָבָה שֶׁלֹּא נֵבוֹשׁ and generous, that we may not be shamed
v'-ha-r'-cha-vah she-lo nei-vosh

וְלֹא נִכָּלֵם לְעוֹלָם וָעֶד: nor humiliated forever.
v'-lo ni-ka-leim l'-olam va-ed.

(On Shabbat add:)

רְצֵה וְהַחֲלִיצֵנוּ May it be Your will that we be strengthened
r'-tzei v'-ha-cha-li-tzeinu

יהוה אֱלֹהֵינוּ בְּמִצְוֹתֶיךָ Adonai our God, in Your commandments,
Adonai Eloheinu b'-mitz-vo-techa

וּבְמִצְוַת and by the commandment
u-v'-mitz-vat

יוֹם הַשְּׁבִיעִי of the seventh day,
yom ha-sh'-vi-i

הַשַּׁבָּת הַגָּדוֹל this great
ha-sha-bat ha-gadol

וְהַקָּדוֹשׁ הַזֶּה and holy Sabbath.
v'-ha-kadosh ha-zeh

כִּי יוֹם זֶה גָּדוֹל וְקָדוֹשׁ Because this day is great and holy
ki yom zeh gadol v'-kadosh

הוּא לְפָנֶיךָ לִשְׁבָּת בּוֹ before You, to cease on it
hu l'-fa-necha lish-bat bo

וְלָנוּחַ בּוֹ בְּאַהֲבָה and rest on it in love
v'-la-nu-ach bo b'-a-ha-vah

כְּמִצְוַת רְצוֹנֶךָ as ordained by Your will.
k'-mitz-vat r'-tzo-necha

וּבִרְצוֹנְךָ הָנִיחַ לָנוּ And by Your will, grant us,
u-vir-tzo-necha ha-ni-ach lanu

יהוה אֱלֹהֵינוּ Adonai our God
Adonai Eloheinu

שֶׁלֹּא תְהֵא צָרָה וְיָגוֹן that there be no distress or sorrow
she-lo t'-hei tza-rah v'-ya-gon

וְאָנָחָה בְּיוֹם מְנוּחָתֵנוּ or sighing on the day of our rest.
va-a-na-cheh b'-yom m'-nu-cha-teinu

וְהַרְאֵנוּ יהוה אֱלֹהֵינוּ Show us, Adonai our God,
v'-har-einu Adonai Eloheinu

בְּנֶחָמַת צִיּוֹן עִירֶךָ the consolation of Zion Your city,
b'-ne-cha-mat Tzi-yon i-recha

וּבְבִנְיַן יְרוּשָׁלַיִם and the rebuilding of Jerusalem,
u-v'-vin-yan Y'-rushalaim

עִיר קָדְשֶׁךָ city of Your sanctuary,
ir kod-she-cha

כִּי אַתָּה הוּא בַּעַל הַיְשׁוּעוֹת for You are the Lord of salvation
ki ata hu ba-al ha-y'-shu-ot

וּבַעַל הַנֶּחָמוֹת: and the Lord of consolation.
u-va-al ha-ne-cha-mot

(On Rosh Chodesh & Yom Tov add:)

אֱלֹהֵינוּ וֵאלֹהֵי אֲבוֹתֵינוּ Our God and God of our fathers,
Eloheinu vei-lo-hei a-vo-tei-nu

יַעֲלֶה וְיָבֹא וְיַגִּיעַ וְיֵרָאֶה may there go up, come, reach, appear,
ya-a-leh v'-yavo v'-yagi-a v'-yei-ra-eh

וְיֵרָצֶה וְיִשָּׁמַע וְיִפָּקֵד be desired and heard, counted
v'-yeira-tzeh v'-yisha-ma v'-yipa-keid

וְיִזָּכֵר זִכְרוֹנֵנוּ and recalled our remembrance
v'-yi-za-cheir zich-ro-neinu

וּפִקְדּוֹנֵנוּ and our reckoning,
u-fik-do-neinu

וְזִכְרוֹן אֲבוֹתֵינוּ and the remembrance of our fathers,
v'-zich-ron a-vo-teinu

וְזִכְרוֹן the remembrance of
v'-zich-ron

מָשִׁיחַ בֶּן דָּוִד עַבְדֶּךָ Messiah son of David Your Servant,
ma-shi-ach ben Da-vid av-decha

וְזִכְרוֹן יְרוּשָׁלַיִם and the remembrance of Jerusalem
v'-zich-ron Y'-ru-sha-la-yim

עִיר קָדְשֶׁךָ city of Your sanctuary,
ir kod-shecha

וְזִכְרוֹן כָּל עַמְּךָ the remembrance of all Your people
v'-zich-ron kol a-mecha

בֵּית יִשְׂרָאֵל לְפָנֶיךָ the house of Israel, before You,
beit Yis-rael l'-fa-ne-cha

לִפְלֵיטָה לְטוֹבָה לְחֵן for survival, well-being, grace,
lif-lei-tah l'-tovah l'-chen

וּלְחֶסֶד וּלְרַחֲמִים לְחַיִּים lovingkindness, compassion, life
u-l'-chesed u-l'-rach-a-mim l'cha-yim

Birchat HaMazon

וּלְשָׁלוֹם בְּיוֹם	and for peace on this day of:	u-l'-shalom b'-yom
רֹאשׁ הַחֹדֶשׁ הַזֶּה	Rosh Chodesh	rosh ha-chodesh ha-zeh
חַג הַמַּצּוֹת הַזֶּה	the Festival of Matzot	chag ha-matzot ha-zeh
חַג הַשָּׁבֻעוֹת הַזֶּה	the Festival of Shavuot	chag ha-sha-vu-ot ha-zeh
חַג הַסֻּכּוֹת הַזֶּה	the Festival of Sukkot	chag ha-sukkot ha-zeh
הַשְּׁמִינִי חַג הָעֲצֶרֶת הַזֶּה	the Festival of Shemini Atzeret	ha-sh'-mini chag ha-a-tzeret ha-zeh
הַזִּכָּרוֹן הַזֶּה	Remembrance (New Year)	ha-zi-ka-ron ha-zeh
זָכְרֵנוּ יהוה אֱלֹהֵינוּ	Remember us Adonai our God	zach-reinu Adonai Eloheinu
בּוֹ לְטוֹבָה וּפָקְדֵנוּ בוֹ	on it for good and be mindful on it	bo l'-tovah u-fak-deinu vo
לִבְרָכָה	for a blessing.	liv-ra-chah
וְהוֹשִׁיעֵנוּ בוֹ לְחַיִּים	Deliver us on it for life	v'-ho-shi-einu vo l'-cha-yim
וּבִדְבַר יְשׁוּעָה	and in accordance with salvation	u-vid-var y'-shu-ah
וְרַחֲמִים חוּס וְחָנֵּנוּ	and compassion, spare and favor us,	v'-ra-chamim chus v'-cha-neinu
וְרַחֵם עָלֵינוּ וְהוֹשִׁיעֵנוּ	and have compassion on us and save us.	v'-ra-chem a-leinu v'-ho-shi-einu
כִּי אֵלֶיךָ עֵינֵינוּ	For to You our eyes are cast	ki ei-lecha ei-neinu
כִּי אֵל מֶלֶךְ חַנּוּן	because You are God, King, Gracious,	ki El melech cha-nun
וְרַחוּם אָתָּה:	and Merciful.	v'-ra-chum ata
וּבְנֵה יְרוּשָׁלַיִם עִיר	Rebuild Jerusalem, city of	u-v'-nei Y'rushalaim ir
הַקֹּדֶשׁ בִּמְהֵרָה בְיָמֵינוּ	the Holy Place speedily in our days.	ha-kodesh bim-hei-rah v'-ya-meinu
בָּרוּךְ אַתָּה יהוה	Blessed are You, Adonai,	Baruch ata Adonai
בּוֹנֶה בְרַחֲמָיו יְרוּשָׁלַיִם	Who, in His mercy, builds Jerusalem.	boneh b'-ra-cha-maiv Y'rushalaim
אָמֵן	Amen.	amen.

Birchat HaMazon

בָּרוּךְ אַתָּה יהוה אֱלֹהֵינוּ Blessed are You, Adonai our God
baruch ata Adonai Eloheinu

מֶלֶךְ הָעוֹלָם הָאֵל אָבִינוּ King of the Universe, God of our fathers,
melech ha-olam ha-El avinu

מַלְכֵּנוּ אַדִּירֵנוּ בּוֹרְאֵנוּ our King, our Mighty One, our Creator,
mal-cheinu a-di-reinu bor-einu

גּוֹאֲלֵנוּ יוֹצְרֵנוּ our Redeemer, our Maker,
go-a-leinu yo-tz'-reinu

קְדוֹשֵׁנוּ קְדוֹשׁ יַעֲקֹב our Holy One, the Holy One of Jacob,
k'-do-sheinu k'-dosh Ya-akov

רוֹעֵנוּ רוֹעֵה יִשְׂרָאֵל our Shepherd, Shepherd of Israel.
ro-einu ro-ei Yis-rael

הַמֶּלֶךְ הַטּוֹב וְהַמֵּטִיב The good King, who does good
ha-melech ha-tov v'-ha-mei-tiv

לַכֹּל שֶׁבְּכָל יוֹם וָיוֹם to all. Every day
la-kol she-b'-chol yom va-yom

הוּא הֵטִיב הוּא מֵטִיב He has done good, He does good,
hu hei-tiv hu mei-tiv

הוּא יֵיטִיב לָנוּ He will do good for us.
hu yei-tiv lanu

הוּא גְמָלָנוּ הוּא גוֹמְלֵנוּ He has rewarded us, He rewards us,
hu g'-ma-lanu hu gom'-leinu

הוּא יִגְמְלֵנוּ לָעַד לְחֵן He will reward us forever with grace,
hu yig-m'-leinu la-ad l'-chen

וּלְחֶסֶד וּלְרַחֲמִים וּלְרֶוַח lovingkindness, compassion, relief,
u-l'-chesed u-l'-ra-chamim u-l'-re-vach

הַצָּלָה וְהַצְלָחָה בְּרָכָה rescue and success, blessing
ha-tza-lah v'-hatz-la-chah b'-ra-chah

וִישׁוּעָה נֶחָמָה and salvation, consolation,
vi-shu-ah ne-cha-mah

פַּרְנָסָה וְכַלְכָּלָה וְרַחֲמִים maintenance, sustenance, compassion
par-na-sah v'-chal-ka-lah v'-ra-chamim

וְחַיִּים וְשָׁלוֹם וְכָל טוֹב and life, peace, and everything good.
v'-cha-yim v'-shalom v'-chol tov

וּמִכָּל טוּב לְעוֹלָם And from all good things forever
u-mi-kol tuv l'-olam

אַל יְחַסְּרֵנוּ: He will not deprive us.
al y'-cha-s'-reinu.

הָרַחֲמָן הוּא יִמְלוֹךְ עָלֵינוּ The Merciful One will reign over us
ha-ra-cha-man hu yim-loch a-leinu

לְעוֹלָם וָעֶד forever and ever.
l'-olam va-ed

הָרַחֲמָן הוּא יִתְבָּרַךְ The Merciful One will be blessed
ha-ra-cha-man hu yit-ba-rach

Birchat HaMazon

בַּשָּׁמַיִם וּבָאָרֶץ in heaven and on earth.
ba-sha-ma-im u-va-aretz

הָרַחֲמָן הוּא יִשְׁתַּבַּח The Merciful One will be praised
ha-ra-cha-man hu yish-ta-bach

לְדוֹר דּוֹרִים וְיִתְפָּאַר through all generations, and glorified
l'-dor do-rim v'-yit-pa-ar

בָּנוּ לָעַד וּלְנֵצַח נְצָחִים in us forever throughout eternity;
banu la-ad u-l'-nei-tzach n'-tza-chim

וְיִתְהַדַּר בָּנוּ לָעַד and honored in us forever
v'-yit-ha-dar banu la-ad

וּלְעוֹלְמֵי עוֹלָמִים and for worlds without end.
u-l'-o-l'-mei o-lamim

הָרַחֲמָן הוּא יְפַרְנְסֵנוּ The Merciful One will maintain us
ha-ra-cha-man hu y'-far-n'-seinu

בְּכָבוֹד with honor.
b'-cha-vod

הָרַחֲמָן הוּא יִשְׁבּוֹר The Merciful One will break
ha-ra-cha-man hu yish-bor

עָלֵנוּ מֵעַל צַוָּארֵנוּ our yoke from upon our necks,
u-leinu mei-al tza-va-reinu

וְהוּא יוֹלִיכֵנוּ קוֹמְמִיּוּת causing us to walk on the heights
v'-hu yo-li-cheinu ko-m'-mi-yut

לְאַרְצֵנוּ of our Land.
l'-ar-tzeinu

הָרַחֲמָן הוּא יִשְׁלַח לָנוּ The Merciful One, may He send for us
ha-ra-cha-man hu yish-lach lanu

בְּרָכָה מְרֻבָּה abundant blessing
b'-ra-chah m'-ru-bah

בַּבַּיִת הַזֶּה וְעַל upon this house, and upon
ba-ba-it ha-zeh v'-al

שֻׁלְחָן זֶה שֶׁאָכַלְנוּ עָלָיו this table upon which we have eaten.
shul-chan ze she-a-chal-nu a-laiv

הָרַחֲמָן הוּא יִשְׁלַח לָנוּ The Merciful One, may He send us
ha-ra-cha-man hu yish-lach lanu

אֶת אֵלִיָּהוּ הַנָּבִיא Elijah the prophet
et Ei-li-ya-hu ha-na-vi

זָכוּר לַטּוֹב who is remembered for good
za-chur la-tov

וִיבַשֶּׂר לָנוּ and who will announce for us
vi-va-ser lanu

בְּשׂוֹרוֹת טוֹבוֹת יְשׁוּעוֹת good tidings of salvation
b'-so-rot tovot y'-shu-ot

וְנֶחָמוֹת and consolations.
v'-ne-cha-mot

Birchat HaMazon

(Guests recite the following: children at parent's table include parentheses)

הָרַחֲמָן הוּא יְבָרֵךְ אֶת
The Merciful One, may He bless
ha-rach-a-man hu y'-va-reich et

(אָבִי מוֹרִי)
(my father, my teacher)
(avi mo-ri)

בַּעַל הַבַּיִת הַזֶּה
the Master of this house,
ba-al ha-ba-it ha-zeh

וְאֶת (אִמִּי מוֹרָתִי)
and (my mother, my teacher),
v'-et (imi mo-rati)

בַּעֲלַת הַבַּיִת הַזֶּה
lady of this house,
ba-a-lat ha-ba-it ha-zeh

אוֹתָם וְאֶת בֵּיתָם
them, their house
otam v'-et bei-tam

וְאֶת זַרְעָם
and their children
v'-et zar-am

וְאֶת כָּל אֲשֶׁר לָהֶם
and all which is theirs—
v'-et kol asher la-hem

(At your own table recite: [include appropriate words in parentheses])

הָרַחֲמָן הוּא יְבָרֵךְ אוֹתִי
The Merciful One, may He bless me,
ha-ra-cha-man hu y'-va-reich oti

(וְאָבִי וְאִמִּי וְאִשְׁתִּי
(and my father, my mother, my wife
(v'-avi v'-imi v'-ish-ti

וְזַרְעִי) וְאֶת כָּל אֲשֶׁר לִי
and my children) and all that is mine—
v'-zar-i) v'-et kol asher li

(All continue here)

אוֹתָנוּ וְאֶת כָּל אֲשֶׁר לָנוּ
ours and all that is ours
o-tanu v'-et kol asher lanu

כְּמוֹ שֶׁנִּתְבָּרְכוּ אֲבוֹתֵינוּ
just as our fathers were blessed,
k'-mo she-nit-bar-chu a-vo-teinu

אַבְרָהָם יִצְחָק וְיַעֲקֹב:
Abraham, Isaac, and Jacob.
Avraham, Yitz-chak v'-Ya-a-kov

בַּכֹּל מִכֹּל
in all things, from all things,
ba-kol mi-kol

כֹּל כֵּן יְבָרֵךְ אוֹתָנוּ
with all things, so may He bless us,
kol chen y'-va-reich o-tanu

כֻּלָּנוּ יַחַד
all of us together as one,
ku-lanu ya-chad

בִּבְרָכָה שְׁלֵמָה
with a complete blessing
biv-ra-chah sh'-lei-mah

וְנֹאמַר אָמֵן:
and let us say, "Amen."
v'-nomar a-mein

Birchat HaMazon

בַּמָּרוֹם יְלַמְּדוּ From on high may they instruct
ba-ma-rom y'-la-m'-du
עֲלֵיהֶם וְעָלֵינוּ זְכוּת them and us of the favorable judgment
a-lei-hem v'-a-leinu z'-chut
שֶׁתְּהֵא לְמִשְׁמֶרֶת שָׁלוֹם by which to guard peace,
she-t'-hei l'-mish-meret shalom
וְנִשָּׂא בְרָכָה מֵאֵת יהוה and may we receive blessing from Adonai
v'-ni-sa v'-ra-cha mei-eit Adonai
וּצְדָקָה מֵאֱלֹהֵי and righteousness from the God
u-tz'-da-kah mei-Elohei
יִשְׁעֵנוּ of our salvation.
yish-ei-nu
וְנִמְצָא חֵן וְשֵׂכֶל טוֹב And may we find grace and good favor
v'-nim-tza chen v'-sei-chel tov
בְּעֵינֵי אֱלֹהִים וְאָדָם: in the eyes of God and man.
b'-ei-nei Elohim v'-a-dam

(On Shabbat add:)

הָרַחֲמָן The Merciful One,
ha-rach-a-man
הוּא יַנְחִילֵנוּ יוֹם may He cause us to inherit the day
hu yan-chi-leinu yom
שֶׁכֻּלוֹ שַׁבָּת which is all Shabbat
she-ku-lo shabbat
וּמְנוּחָה and a rest (reflecting)
u-m'-nu-chah
לְחַיֵּי הָעוֹלָמִים eternal life.
l'-cha-yei ha-o-lamim

(On Rosh Chodesh)

הָרַחֲמָן הוּא יְחַדֵּשׁ The Merciful One, may He renew
ha-ra-cha-man hu y'-cha-deish
עָלֵינוּ אֶת הַחֹדֶשׁ הַזֶּה upon us this month
a-leinu et ha-chodesh ha-zeh
לְטוֹבָה וְלִבְרָכָה for good and for blessing
l'-tovah v'-liv-ra-chah

(On Yom Tov)

הָרַחֲמָן The Merciful One,
ha-ra-cha-man
הוּא יַנְחִילֵנוּ may He cause us to inherit
hu yan-chi-leinu
יוֹם שֶׁכֻּלוֹ טוֹב a day which is completely good.
yom she-ku-lo tov

Birchat HaMazon

(On Rosh HaShanah)

הָרַחֲמָן הוּא יְחַדֵּשׁ עָלֵינוּ The Merciful One, may He renew for us
ha-ra-cha-man hu y'-cha-deish a-leinu

אֶת הַשָּׁנָה הַזֹּאת לְטוֹבָה this year for good
et ha-sha-nah ha-zot l'-to-vah

וְלִבְרָכָה and for blessing
v'-liv-ra-chah

(On Sukkot)

הָרַחֲמָן הוּא יָקִים The Merciful One, may He raise up
ha-ra-cha-man hu ya-kim

לָנוּ אֶת סֻכַּת דָּוִד הַנּוֹפָלֶת for us the fallen sukkah of David
lanu et sukkat Da-vid ha-no-fa-let

הָרַחֲמָן הוּא יְזַכֵּנוּ The Merciful One, may He prepare us
ha-ra-cha-man hu y'-za-keinu

לִימוֹת הַמָּשִׁיחַ for the days of the Messiah
li-mot ha-ma-shi-ach

וּלְחַיֵּי הָעוֹלָם הַבָּא and for life in the world to come.
u-l'-cha-yei ha-o-lam ha-ba

מַגְדִּיל יְשׁוּעוֹת מַלְכּוֹ He who gives deliverance to His king
mag-dil y'-shu-ot mal-ko

(On Shabbat and Yom Tov)

מִגְדּוֹל יְשׁוּעוֹת He who is a tower of salvation
mig-dol y'-shu-ot

מַלְכּוֹ to His king
mal-ko

וְעֹשֶׂה חֶסֶד and does lovingkindness
v'-o-seh chesed

לִמְשִׁיחוֹ לְדָוִד to His anointed, to David
lim-shi-cho l'-Da-vid

וּלְזַרְעוֹ עַד עוֹלָם: and to his Seed forever.[1]
u-l'-zar-o ad o-lam

עֹשֶׂה שָׁלוֹם בִּמְרוֹמָיו He who makes peace in His heights
o-seh shalom bim-ro-maiv

הוּא יַעֲשֶׂה שָׁלוֹם עָלֵינוּ May He make peace upon us
hu ya-a-seh shalom a-leinu

וְעַל כָּל יִשְׂרָאֵל and upon all Israel[2]
v'-al kol Yis-rael

וְאִמְרוּ אָמֵן: and let us say, Amen.
v'-im-ru a-mein

(1) 2Sam 22:51 (2) Job 25:2

Birchat HaMazon

יְראוּ אֶת יהוה קְדוֹשָׁיו	Fear Adonai, you His holy ones,	y'-ru et Adonai k'-do-shaiv
כִּי אֵין מַחְסוֹר	because there is no lack	ki ein mach-sor
לִירֵאָיו:[1]	to those who fear Him[1]	li-rei-av
כְּפִירִים רָשׁוּ וְרָעֵבוּ	Young lions may feel want and hunger	k'-fi-rim ra-shu v'-ra-ei-vu
וְדוֹרְשֵׁי יהוה	but those who seek Adonai	v'-do-r'-shei Adonai
לֹא יַחְסְרוּ כָל טוֹב:[2]	lack nothing of all things good.[2]	lo yach-s'-ru chol tov
הוֹדוּ לַיהוה כִּי טוֹב	Give thanks to Adonai for He is good,	ho-du la-Adonai ki tov
כִּי לְעוֹלָם חַסְדּוֹ:[3]	for His lovingkindness is eternal.[3]	ki l'-o-lam chas-do
פּוֹתֵחַ אֶת יָדֶךָ וּמַשְׂבִּיעַ	You open Your hand and satisfy	po-tei-ach et ya-decha u-mas-bi-a
לְכָל חַי רָצוֹן:[4]	the desire of every living thing.[4]	l'-chol chai ra-tzon
בָּרוּךְ הַגֶּבֶר	Blessed is the man	baruch ha-gever
אֲשֶׁר יִבְטַח בַּיהוה	who trusts in Adonai,	asher yiv-tach ba-Adonai
וְהָיָה יהוה מִבְטַחוֹ:[5]	and Adonai will be his security.[5]	v'-ha-yah Adonai miv-ta-cho
נַעַר הָיִיתִי גַּם זָקַנְתִּי	I was young, and I have grown old	na-ar ha-yi-ti gam za-kan-ti
וְלֹא רָאִיתִי	and I have not seen	v'-lo ra-i-ti
צַדִּיק נֶעֱזָב	a righteous one forsaken	tza-dik ne-e-zav
וְזַרְעוֹ מְבַקֶּשׁ לָחֶם:[6]	nor his seed begging for bread.[6]	v'-zar-o m'-va-keish la-chem
יהוה עֹז לְעַמּוֹ יִתֵּן	Adonai will give strength to His people,	Adonai oz l'-amo yi-tein
יהוה יְבָרֵךְ	Adonai will bless	Adonai y'-va-reich
אֶת עַמּוֹ בַשָּׁלוֹם:[7]	His people with peace.[7]	et a-mo ba-shalom

(1) Ps 34:10-11 (2) Ps 136:1 (3) Ps 145:16 (4) Jer 17:7 (5) Ps 37:35
(6) Ps 37:25 (7) Ps 29:11

Shabbat Morning Service

עֲטִיפַת טַלִּית Putting on the Tallit

(inspect the tzitzit and and recite:)

בָּרְכִי נַפְשִׁי אֶת יהוה My soul, Bless Adonai!
bar-chi naf-shi et Adonai

יהוה אֱלֹהַי גָּדַלְתָּ מְּאֹד Adonai my God, You are very great!
Adonai Elohai ga-dal-ta m'-od

הוֹד וְהָדָר לָבָשְׁתָּ: With beauty and splendor are You clothed;
Hod v'-ha-dar la-vash-ta

עֹטֶה אוֹר כַּשַּׂלְמָה Enrapped in light as with a garment;
o-teh or ka-sal-mah

נוֹטֶה שָׁמַיִם כַּיְרִיעָה:[1] You spread out the heavens like a curtain.[1]
no-te sha-ma-im ka-y'-ri-ah

(hold the tallit in readiness to wrap around yourself, and recite the blessing:)

בָּרוּךְ אַתָּה יהוה אֱלֹהֵינוּ Blessed are You, Adonai our God
ba-ruch a-tah Adonai Eloheinu

מֶלֶךְ הָעוֹלָם King of the Universe
melech ha-o-lam

אֲשֶׁר קִדְּשָׁנוּ בְּמִצְוֹתָיו Who sanctified us with His commandments
a-sher ki-d'-sha-nu b'-mitz-vo-tav

וְצִוָּנוּ לְהִתְעַטֵּף and commanded us to wrap ourselves
v'-tzi-va-nu l'-hit-a-teif

בַּצִּיצִית: with tzitzit.
ba-tzi-tzit.

(put the tallit over the head, wrapping it around you completely, and continue:)

מַה יָּקָר חַסְדְּךָ How precious is Your lovingkindness,
ma ya-kar chas-d'-cha

אֱלֹהִים וּבְנֵי אָדָם בְּצֵל O God, even mankind, in the shadow
Elohim u-v'-nei a-dam b'-tzeil

כְּנָפֶיךָ יֶחֱסָיוּן: יִרְוְיֻן of Your wings, takes refuge. They drink
k'-na-fe-cha ye-che-sa-yun yir-v'-yun

מִדֶּשֶׁן בֵּיתֶךָ from the abundance of Your house,
mi-de-shen bei-te-cha

וְנַחַל עֲדָנֶיךָ and from the river of Your delights
v'-na-chal a-da-ne-cha

תַשְׁקֵם: You give them drink.
tash-kem

כִּי עִמְּךָ מְקוֹר חַיִּים For with You is the fountain of life;
ki i-m'-cha m'-kor cha-yim

בְּאוֹרְךָ נִרְאֶה אוֹר: in Your light we see light.
b'-o-r'-cha nir-eh or.

(1) Isaiah 40:22

Shabbat Morning Service

מְשֹׁךְ חַסְדְּךָ	Continue Your lovingkindness
	m'-shoch chas-d'-cha
לְיֹדְעֶיךָ	to those who know You,
	l'-yod-echa
וְצִדְקָתְךָ	and Your righteousness
	v'-tzid-ka-t'-cha
לְיִשְׁרֵי לֵב: [1]	to the upright of heart.[1]
	l'-yish-rei leiv

תפלת שחרית Morning Prayers

Upon entering the place of prayer, the following verses of Scripture are recited as we approach our King and seek His presence.

מַה טֹּבוּ אֹהָלֶיךָ יַעֲקֹב	How good are your tents, Jacob:
	ma to-vu o-ha-le-cha Ya-a-kov,
מִשְׁכְּנֹתֶיךָ יִשְׂרָאֵל [2]	Your dwelling places, O Israel.[2]
	mish-k'-no-te-cha Yis-ra-eil.
וַאֲנִי בְּרֹב	As for me, in the abundance of
	va-a-ni b'-rov
חַסְדְּךָ אָבוֹא	Your lovingkindness I will enter
	chas-d'-cha a-vo
בֵיתֶךָ אֶשְׁתַּחֲוֶה אֶל	Your house, I will prostrate myself toward
	vei-te-cha esh-ta-cha-veh el
הֵיכַל קָדְשְׁךָ בְּיִרְאָתֶךָ [3]	Your Holy Sanctuary in awe of You.[3]
	hei-chal kod-sh'-cha b'-yir-a-te-cha.
יהוה אָהַבְתִּי מְעוֹן בֵּיתֶךָ	Adonai, I love the dwelling of Your house,
	Adonai a-hav-ti m'-on bei-te-cha
וּמְקוֹם מִשְׁכַּן כְּבוֹדֶךָ [4]	even the place where Your glory resides.[4]
	u-m'-kom mish-kan k'-vo-de-cha
וַאֲנִי אֶשְׁתַּחֲוֶה	As for me, I will prostrate myself
	va-a-ni esh-ta-cha-veh
וְאֶכְרָעָה אֶבְרְכָה לִפְנֵי	and bow, I will kneel before
	v'-ech-ra-a ev-r'-cha lif-nei
יהוה עֹשִׂי וַאֲנִי תְפִלָּתִי	Adonai my Maker. As for me, may my prayer
	Adonai o-si va-a-ni t'-fi-la-ti
לְךָ יהוה עֵת רָצוֹן	to You Adonai, be at an acceptable time.
	l'-cha Adonai eit ratz-on
אֱלֹהִים בְּרָב	O God, in the abundance of
	Elohim be-rov
חַסְדְּךָ עֲנֵנִי	Your lovingkindness, answer me
	chas-de-cha a-nei-ni
בֶּאֱמֶת יִשְׁעֶךָ [5]	with the truth of Your salvation.[5]
	be-e-met yish-e-cha

(1) Ps 36:10 (2) Num 24:5 - Some interpret Billam's words as describing houses of worship [b.*Sanhedrin* 105a] (3) Ps 5:8 (4) Ps 26:8 (5) Ps 69:14[13]

Shabbat Morning Service

The *Chazzan* says:

בָּרְכוּ אֶת יהוה
הַמְבֹרָךְ:

Bless Adonai
Ba-r'-chu et Adonai
Who is blessed!
ha-m'-vorach.

Congregation responds:

בָּרוּךְ יהוה הַמְבֹרָךְ
לְעוֹלָם וָעֶד:

Blessed is Adonai, Who is blessed
Baruch Adonai ha-m'-vorach
forever and ever.
l'-o-lam va-ed.

ברכות קריאת שמע

The Blessings of the Shema

Congregation and Chazzan

בָּרוּךְ אַתָּה יהוה
אֱלֹהֵינוּ מֶלֶךְ הָעוֹלָם
יוֹצֵר אוֹר וּבוֹרֵא חֹשֶׁךְ
עֹשֶׂה שָׁלוֹם
וּבוֹרֵא אֶת הַכֹּל:

Blessed are You, Adonai
Baruch ata Adonai
our God, King of the universe
Eloheinu melech ha-olam
Former of the light and Creator of darkness,
yo-tzeir or u-vo-rei cho-shech
Maker of peace
o-seh shalom
and Creator of everything.
u-vo-rei et ha-kol

Chazzan

אַהֲבָה רַבָּה אֲהַבְתָּנוּ
יהוה אֱלֹהֵינוּ
חֶמְלָה גְדוֹלָה וִיתֵרָה
חָמַלְתָּ עָלֵינוּ
אָבִינוּ מַלְכֵּנוּ
בַּעֲבוּר אֲבוֹתֵינוּ
שֶׁבָּטְחוּ בְךָ
וַתְּלַמְּדֵם חֻקֵּי חַיִּים

With much love You have loved us,
A-hava raba a-hav-tanu
Adonai, our God;
Adonai Eloheinu
With great and abundant pity
chem-la g'-dola vi-tei-ra
You have pitied us.
cha-mal-ta aleinu.
Our Father, our King,
Avinu mal-cheinu
for the sake of our fathers
ba-avur avo-teinu
who trusted in You,
she-ba-t'-chu v'-cha
and You taught them the statutes of life;
va-t'-la-m'-deim chu-kei chayim

Shabbat Morning Service

כֵּן תְּחָנֵּנוּ וּתְלַמְּדֵנוּ so too be gracious to us and teach us.
ken t'-cha-neinu u-t'-la-m'-deinu

אָבִינוּ הָאָב הָרַחֲמָן Our Father, compassionate Father,
avinu ha-av ha-ra-cha-man

הַמְרַחֵם Who acts with compassion;
ha-m'-ra-chem

רַחֵם עָלֵינוּ have compassion upon us
ra-chem a-leinu

וְתֵן בְּלִבֵּנוּ לְהָבִין and put into our hearts to understand
v'ten b'-li-beinu l'-ha-vin

וּלְהַשְׂכִּיל and to comprehend,
u-l'-has-kil

לִשְׁמֹעַ לִלְמֹד וּלְלַמֵּד to listen, learn and teach,
lish-mo-a lil-mod u-l'-la-med

לִשְׁמֹר וְלַעֲשׂוֹת וּלְקַיֵּם to guard, to perform, and fulfill
lish-mor v'-la-a-sot u-l'-ka-yem

אֶת כָּל דִּבְרֵי תַלְמוּד all the words of instruction in
et kol div-rei tal-mud

תוֹרָתֶךָ בְּאַהֲבָה Your Torah with love.
to-ra-techa b'-a-ha-vah

וְהָאֵר עֵינֵינוּ בְּתוֹרָתֶךָ Enlighten our eyes in Your Torah
v'-ha-eir ei-neinu b'-to-ra-techa

וְדַבֵּק לִבֵּנוּ and cause our hearts to cleave
v'-da-beik li-beinu

בְּמִצְוֹתֶיךָ to Your commandments.
b'-mitz-vo-techa

וְיַחֵד לְבָבֵנוּ לְאַהֲבָה Unify our hearts to love
v'-ya-cheid l'-va-veinu l'-a-ha-vah

וּלְיִרְאָה אֶת שְׁמֶךָ and to fear Your Name,
u-l'-yir-ah et sh'-mecha

וְלֹא נֵבוֹשׁ לְעוֹלָם וָעֶד: and may we never be put to shame,
v'-lo nei-vosh l'-olam va-ed

כִּי בְשֵׁם קָדְשְׁךָ הַגָּדוֹל because in Your holy, great,
ki v'-shem kod-sh'-cha ha-gadol

וְהַנּוֹרָא בָּטָחְנוּ and awesome Name have we trusted.
v'-ha-no-ra ba-tach-nu

נָגִילָה וְנִשְׂמְחָה May we exult and rejoice
na-gi-lah v'-nis-m'-chah

בִּישׁוּעָתֶךָ in Your salvation.
bi-shu-a-techa

וַהֲבִיאֵנוּ לְשָׁלוֹם Bring us in peace
va-ha-vi-einu l'-shalom

מֵאַרְבַּע כַּנְפוֹת הָאָרֶץ from the four corners of the earth
mei-ar-ba kan-fot ha-aretz

Shabbat Morning Service

וְתוֹלִיכֵנוּ קוֹמְמִיּוּת לְאַרְצֵנוּ and lead us to our Land in honor,
v'-to-li-cheinu ko-m'-mi-yut l'-ar-tzeinu

כִּי אֵל פּוֹעֵל because You are God Who makes
ki El po-el

יְשׁוּעוֹת אָתָּה salvation,
y'-shu-ot ata

וּבָנוּ בָחַרְתָּ מִכָּל עַם and You have chosen us from all peoples
u-vanu va-char-ta mi-kol am

וְלָשׁוֹן וְקֵרַבְתָּנוּ and tongues, and brought us close
v'-la-shon v'-kei-rav-tanu

לְשִׁמְךָ הַגָּדוֹל סֶלָה בֶּאֱמֶת to Your great Name forever in truth,
l'-shim-cha ha-gadol se-lah be-emet

לְהוֹדוֹת לְךָ to offer You thanksgiving
l'-ho-dot l'-cha

וּלְיַחֶדְךָ בְּאַהֲבָה and to declare Your oneness with love.
u-l'-ya-ched-cha b'-a-ha-vah

בָּרוּךְ אַתָּה יהוה הַבּוֹחֵר Blessed are You, Adonai, Who chooses
baruch ata Adonai ha-bo-cheir

בְּעַמּוֹ יִשְׂרָאֵל בְּאַהֲבָה His people Israel with love.
b'-amo Yis-rael b'a-ha-vah

שמע The Shema

Congregation stands and recites:
(It is traditional to close or cover the eyes when praying the Shema.)

שְׁמַע יִשְׂרָאֵל **Hear,** O Israel,
Shema Yisrael

יהוה אֱלֹהֵינוּ יהוה אֶחָד: Adonai is our God, Adonai is one!
Adonai Eloheinu Adonai echad

בָּרוּךְ שֵׁם כְּבוֹד Blessed is the Name! The glory of
baruch shem k'vod

מַלְכוּתוֹ לְעוֹלָם וָעֶד His kingdom is for ever and ever.
mal-chuto l'-olam va-ed

וְאָהַבְתָּ אֵת יהוה אֱלֹהֶיךָ **And you shall love** Adonai Your God
v'-a-hav-ta et Adonai Elohei-cha

בְּכָל־לְבָבְךָ וּבְכָל־נַפְשְׁךָ with all your heart and with all your soul
b'-chol l'-vav-cha u-v'-chol naf-sh'-cha

וּבְכָל־מְאֹדֶךָ and with all your might.
u-v'-chol m'-o-decha

וְהָיוּ הַדְּבָרִים הָאֵלֶּה אֲשֶׁר These words which
v'-ha-yu ha-d'-va-rim ha-ei-le asher

אָנֹכִי מְצַוְּךָ הַיּוֹם I command you today shall be
a-nochi m'-tza-v'-cha ha-yom

עַל־לְבָבֶךָ: on your heart.
al l'-va-vecha

Shabbat Morning Service

וְשִׁנַּנְתָּם	And you shall teach them diligently	v'-shi-nan-tam
לְבָנֶיךָ וְדִבַּרְתָּ בָּם	to your children and speak of them	l'-va-necha v'-di-bar-ta bam
בְּשִׁבְתְּךָ בְּבֵיתֶךָ	when you sit in your house,	b'-shiv-t'-cha b'-vei-techa
וּבְלֶכְתְּךָ בַדֶּרֶךְ	when you travel on the road,	u-v'-lech-t'-cha va-derech
וּבְשָׁכְבְּךָ וּבְקוּמֶךָ	and when you lie down and rise up.	u-v'-shoch-b'-cha u-v'-ku-mecha
וּקְשַׁרְתָּם לְאוֹת	Bind them for a sign	u-k'-shar-tam l'-ot
עַל־יָדֶךָ וְהָיוּ	upon your hand and they shall be	al ya-decha v'-ha-yu
לְטֹטָפֹת בֵּין עֵינֶיךָ	for *tefillin* between your eyes;	l'-to-ta-fot bein ei-neicha
וּכְתַבְתָּם עַל מְזֻזֹת בֵּיתֶךָ	and write them upon the doorposts	u-ch'-tav-tam al m'-zu-zot
וּבִשְׁעָרֶיךָ:	of your house and upon your gates.[1]	bei-techa u-vish-a-reicha

וְהָיָה אִם־שָׁמֹעַ תִּשְׁמְעוּ	**And it shall be** if you diligently obey[2]	v'-ha-yah im sha-mo-a tish-m'-u
אֶל־מִצְוֹתַי אֲשֶׁר אָנֹכִי מְצַוֶּה	My commandments which I	el mitz-vo-taiv asher a-no-chi
אֶתְכֶם הַיּוֹם	am commanding you today,	m'-tza-veh et-chem ha-yom
לְאַהֲבָה אֶת יְהוָה	to love Adonai	l'-a-ha-vah et Adonai
אֱלֹהֵיכֶם וּלְעָבְדוֹ	Your God and to serve Him	Elohei-chem u-l'-av-do
בְּכָל־לְבַבְכֶם	with all your heart	b'-chol l'-vav-chem
וּבְכָל־נַפְשְׁכֶם וְנָתַתִּי	and with all your soul, that I will give	u-v'-chol naf-sh'-chem v'-na-ta-ti
מְטַר־אַרְצְכֶם בְּעִתּוֹ	rain for your Land in its proper time,	m'-tar ar-tz'-chem b'-ito
יוֹרֶה וּמַלְקוֹשׁ	the early and late rain	yo-reh u-mal-kosh
וְאָסַפְתָּ דְגָנֶךָ	that you may gather in your grain,	v'-a-saf-ta d'-ga-necha
וְתִירֹשְׁךָ וְיִצְהָרֶךָ	your wine, and your oil.	v' tir-sh'-cha v'-yitz-ha-recha

(1) Deut 6:4ff (2) Deut 11:13ff

Shabbat Morning Service

וְנָתַתִּי עֵשֶׂב בְּשָׂדְךָ
And I will give grass in your field
v'-na-tati ei-sev b'-sa-d'-cha

לִבְהֶמְתֶּךָ
for your cattle,
liv-hem-techa

וְאָכַלְתָּ וְשָׂבָעְתָּ
and you will eat and be satisfied.
v'-a-chal-ta v'-sa-vata

הִשָּׁמְרוּ לָכֶם
Guard yourselves
hi-sha-m'-ru la-chem

פֶּן־יִפְתֶּה לְבַבְכֶם
lest your heart be swayed
pen yif-teh l'-vav-chem

וְסַרְתֶּם וַעֲבַדְתֶּם
and you go astray and serve
v'-sar-tem va-a-vad-tem

אֱלֹהִים אֲחֵרִים
other gods
elohim a-chei-rim

וְהִשְׁתַּחֲוִיתֶם לָהֶם
and bow down to them.
v'-hish-ta-cha-vi-tem la-hem

וְחָרָה אַף־יהוה
Then the wrath of Adonai will blaze
v'-cha-rah af Adonai

בָּכֶם וְעָצַר
against you and He will close off
ba-chem v'-a-tzar

אֶת־הַשָּׁמַיִם וְלֹא־יִהְיֶה
the heavens and there will be no
et ha-sha-mayim v'-lo yih-yeh

מָטָר וְהָאֲדָמָה לֹא תִתֵּן
rain and the ground will not give forth
ma-tar v'-ha-a-damah lo ti-ten

אֶת־יְבוּלָהּ וַאֲבַדְתֶּם
its produce and you will perish
et y'-vulah va-a-vad-tem

מְהֵרָה מֵעַל הָאָרֶץ הַטֹּבָה
quickly from the good Land
m'-hei-rah mei-al ha-aretz ha-tovah

אֲשֶׁר יהוה נֹתֵן לָכֶם:
which Adonai is giving to you.
asher Adonai no-tein la-chem

וְשַׂמְתֶּם אֶת דְּבָרַי אֵלֶּה
Place these words of Mine
v'-sam-tem et d'-va-rai ei-leh

עַל־לְבַבְכֶם וְעַל־נַפְשְׁכֶם
upon your heart and upon your soul
al l'-vav-chem v'-al naf-sh'-chem

וּקְשַׁרְתֶּם אֹתָם לְאוֹת
and bind them for a sign
u-k'-shar-tem o-tam l'-ot

עַל־יֶדְכֶם וְהָיוּ
upon your hand and they shall be
al yed-chem v'-ha-yu

לְטוֹטָפֹת בֵּין עֵינֵיכֶם:
tefillin between your eyes.
l'-to-ta-fot bein ei-nei-chem

וְלִמַּדְתֶּם אֹתָם אֶת־בְּנֵיכֶם
Teach them to your children
v'-li-mad-tem o-tam et b'-nei-chem

לְדַבֵּר בָּם בְּשִׁבְתְּךָ
to discuss them while you sit
l'-da-beir bam b'-shiv-t'-cha

בְּבֵיתֶךָ וּבְלֶכְתְּךָ
in your home and when you travel
b'-vei-techa u-v'-lech-t'-cha

Shabbat Morning Service

בַּדֶּרֶךְ וּבְשָׁכְבְּךָ	on the road, and when you lie down	ba-derech u-v'-shoch-b'-cha
וּבְקוּמֶךָ:	and when you rise up.	u-v'-ku-mecha
וּכְתַבְתָּם עַל־מְזוּזוֹת	You shall write them on the doorposts	u-ch'-tav-tam al m'-zu-zot
בֵּיתֶךָ וּבִשְׁעָרֶיךָ:	of your house and on your gates,	bei-techa u'-vish-a-recha
לְמַעַן יִרְבּוּ יְמֵיכֶם	in order to prolong your days	l'-ma-an yir-bu y'-mei-chem
וִימֵי בְנֵיכֶם	and the days of your children	vi-mei v'-nei-chem
עַל הָאֲדָמָה אֲשֶׁר	upon the ground which	al ha-a-da-mah asher
נִשְׁבַּע יהוה לַאֲבֹתֵיכֶם	Adonai swore by oath to your fathers	nish-ba Adonai la-a-vo-tei-chem
לָתֵת לָהֶם כִּימֵי	to give them, like the days of	la-teit la-hem ki-mei
הַשָּׁמַיִם עַל־הָאָרֶץ:[1]	the heavens upon the earth.[1]	ha-sha-mayim al ha-aretz
וַיֹּאמֶר יהוה אֶל־מֹשֶׁה	**And Adonai spoke** to Moses	va-yomer Adonai el Moshe
לֵּאמֹר: דַּבֵּר אֶל־בְּנֵי	saying: Speak to the children of	lei-mor da-beir el b'-nei
יִשְׂרָאֵל וְאָמַרְתָּ אֲלֵהֶם:	Israel and say to them	Yis-rael v'-a-marta a-lei-hem
וְעָשׂוּ לָהֶם	that they should make for themselves	v'-asu la-hem
צִיצִת עַל־כַּנְפֵי בִגְדֵיהֶם	*tzitzit* upon the corners of their garments	tzi-tzit al kan-fei vig-dei-hem
לְדֹרֹתָם	throughout their generations.	l'-do-ro-tam
וְנָתְנוּ עַל־צִיצִת	And they shall put upon the *tzitzit*	v'-na-t'-nu al tzi-tzit
הַכָּנָף פְּתִיל תְּכֵלֶת	of each corner a thread of *techeilet*	ha-ka-naf p'-til t'-chei-let
וְהָיָה לָכֶם לְצִיצִת	that it may be *tzitzit* for you,	v'-ha-yah la-chem l'-tzi-tzit
וּרְאִיתֶם אֹתוֹ וּזְכַרְתֶּם	that you may see it and remember	u-r'-item oto u-z'-char-tem
אֶת־כָּל־מִצְוֹת יהוה	all the commandments of Adonai	et kol mitz-vot Adonai
וַעֲשִׂיתֶם אֹתָם	and do them,	va-a-si-tem o-tam

(1) Deut 11:13ff

Shabbat Morning Service

וְלֹא תָתוּרוּ — so that you will not turn aside
v'-lo ta-turu

אַחֲרֵי לְבַבְכֶם וְאַחֲרֵי — after your hearts and after
a-cha-rei l'-vav-chem v'-a-charei

עֵינֵיכֶם אֲשֶׁר־אַתֶּם — your eyes which cause you
ei-nei-chem asher a-tem

זֹנִים אַחֲרֵיהֶם: — to act in unfaithfulness after them.
zo-nim a-cha-rei-hem

לְמַעַן תִּזְכְּרוּ וַעֲשִׂיתֶם — Therefore you will remember and do
l'-ma-an tiz-k'-ru va-a-si-tem

אֶת־כָּל־מִצְוֹתָי — all My commandments
et kol mitz-vo-tai

וִהְיִיתֶם קְדֹשִׁים לֵאלֹהֵיכֶם: — and you will be holy to your God.
vih-yi-tem k'-doshim lei-lo-heichem

אֲנִי יהוה אֱלֹהֵיכֶם אֲשֶׁר — I am Adonai your God Who
ani Adonai Elohei-chem asher

הוֹצֵאתִי אֶתְכֶם מֵאֶרֶץ — brought you out from the land
ho-tzei-ti et-chem mei-eretz

מִצְרַיִם לִהְיוֹת לָכֶם — of Eygpt to be your
mitz-ra-im lih-yot la-chem

לֵאלֹהִים אֲנִי יהוה — God. I am Adonai
lei-lohim ani Adonai

אֱלֹהֵיכֶם:[1] — your God.[1]
Elohei-chem

Chazzan continues alone

יהוה אֱלֹהֵיכֶם אֱמֶת — Adonai Your God is true—
Adonai Elohei-chem emet

אֱמֶת וְיַצִּיב וְנָכוֹן — true and firm, certain
v'-ya-tziv v'-na-chon

וְקַיָּם וְיָשָׁר וְנֶאֱמָן — and enduring, upright and faithful,
v'-ka-yam v'-ya-shar v'-ne-e-man

וְאָהוּב וְחָבִיב — beloved and cherished,
v'-a-huv v'-cha-viv

וְנֶחְמָד וְנָעִים — desired and pleasant,
v'-nech-mad v'-na-im

וְנוֹרָא וְאַדִּיר — awesome and mighty,
v'-no-ra v'-adir

וּמְתֻקָּן וּמְקֻבָּל — correct and accepted,
u-m'-tu-kan u-m'-ku-bal

וְטוֹב וְיָפֶה הַדָּבָר הַזֶּה — good and beautiful is this word
v'-tov v'-ya-feh ha-davar ha-zeh

(1) Num 15:37-41

Shabbat Morning Service

עָלֵינוּ לְעוֹלָם וָעֶד for us for all eternity.
a-leinu l'-o-lam va-ed.

אֱמֶת אֱלֹהֵי עוֹלָם It is true, the God of the universe
emet Elohei o-lam

מַלְכֵּנוּ צוּר יַעֲקֹב is our King, the stronghold of Jacob
mal-kei-nu tzur Ya-akov

מָגֵן יִשְׁעֵנוּ is the shield of our salvation.
ma-gein yish-einu

לְדֹר וָדֹר Throughout all generations
l'-dor va-dor

הוּא קַיָּם וּשְׁמוֹ קַיָּם He endures and His Name endures;
hu ka-yam u-sh'-mo ka-yam

וְכִסְאוֹ נָכוֹן His throne is confirmed
v'-chis-o na-chon

וּמַלְכוּתוֹ וֶאֱמוּנָתוֹ and His sovereignty and His faithfulness
u-mal-chuto ve-emu-na-to

לָעַד קַיָּמֶת endure forever.
la-ad ka-ya-met

Chazzan continues

עַל הָרִאשׁוֹנִים Upon the former generations
al ha-rish-o-nim

וְעַל הָאַחֲרוֹנִים and upon the latter generations
v'-al ha-a-cha-ro-nim

דָּבָר טוֹב וְקַיָּם לְעוֹלָם וָעֶד this word is good and enduring forever.
davar tov v'-ka-yam l'-o-lam va-ed

אֱמֶת וֶאֱמוּנָה חֹק True and faithful is this statute
emet ve-e-mun-ah chok

וְלֹא יַעֲבֹר and it will not pass away.
v'-lo ya-a-vor

אֱמֶת שָׁאַתָּה הוּא יהוה Truly You, Adonai, are
emet sha-a-tah hu Adonai

אֱלֹהֵינוּ וֵאלֹהֵי אֲבוֹתֵינוּ our God and the God of our fathers,
Eloheinu vei-lohei a-vo-teinu

מַלְכֵּנוּ מֶלֶךְ אֲבוֹתֵינוּ our King, the King of our fathers,
mal-keinu melech a-vo-teinu

גֹּאֲלֵנוּ גֹּאֵל אֲבוֹתֵינוּ our Redeemer, Redeemer of our fathers,
go-a-leinu go-eil a-vo-teinu

יוֹצְרֵנוּ צוּר יְשׁוּעָתֵינוּ our Creator, Rock of our Salvation
yo-tz'-reinu tzur y'-shu-a-teinu

פּוֹדֵנוּ וּמַצִּילֵנוּ our Liberator and Deliverer.
po-deinu u-ma-tzi-leinu

מֵעוֹלָם שְׁמֶךָ Your Name is from eternity
mei-olam sh'-mecha

Shabbat Morning Service

אֵין אֱלֹהִים זוּלָתֶךָ — There is no God but You.
ein Elohim zu-la-techa

Chazzan continues

עֶזְרַת אֲבוֹתֵינוּ — The help of our fathers
ez-rat a-vo-teinu

אַתָּה הוּא מֵעוֹלָם — You have been from all eternity,
ata hu mei-o-lam

מָגֵן וּמוֹשִׁיעַ לִבְנֵיהֶם — a Shield and Savior for their children
ma-gein u-mo-shi-a liv-neihem

אַחֲרֵיהֶם בְּכָל דּוֹר וָדוֹר — after them in every generation.
a-cha-reihem b'-chol dor va-dor

בְּרוּם עוֹלָם — The heights of the universe
b'-rum o-lam

מוֹשָׁבֶךָ וּמִשְׁפָּטֶךָ — is Your abode, and Your judgments
mo-sha-vecha u-mish-pa-techa

וְצִדְקָתְךָ עַד — and Your righteousness reach
v'-tzid-ka-t'-cha ad

אַפְסֵי אָרֶץ — to the ends of the earth.
af-sei aretz

אַשְׁרֵי אִישׁ שֶׁיִּשְׁמַע — Blessed is the person who obeys
ash-rei ish she-yish-ma

לְמִצְוֹתֶיךָ וְתוֹרָתְךָ — Your commandments, and Your Torah
l'-mitz-vo-techa v'-to-ra-t'cha

וּדְבָרְךָ יָשִׂים עַל לִבּוֹ — and Your word he places on his heart.
u-d'-va-r'-cha ya-sim al li-bo

אֱמֶת אַתָּה הוּא אָדוֹן — Truly you are the Master
emet ata hu adon

לְעַמֶּךָ וּמֶלֶךְ גִּבּוֹר — of Your people and a mighty King
l'-a-me-cha u-melech gi-bor

לָרִיב רִיבָם — to plead their case.
la-riv ri-vam

אֱמֶת אַתָּה הוּא רִאשׁוֹן — Truly You are the first
emet ata hu rishon

וְאַתָּה הוּא אַחֲרוֹן וּמִבַּלְעָדֶיךָ — and You are the last and beside You
v'-ata hu a-cha-ron umi-bal-a-deicha

אֵין לָנוּ מֶלֶךְ גּוֹאֵל — we have no king, redeemer,
ein lanu melech go-eil

וּמוֹשִׁיעַ מִמִּצְרַיִם — nor savior. From Egypt
u-mo-shi-a mi-mitz-ra-im

גְּאַלְתָּנוּ יהוה אֱלֹהֵינוּ — You redeemed us, Adonai, our God
g'-al-tanu Adonai Eloheinu

וּמִבֵּית עֲבָדִים — and from the house of slavery
u-mi-beit a-vadim

Shabbat Morning Service

פְּדִיתָנוּ כָּל בְּכוֹרֵיהֶם	You freed us. All their firstborn	p'-di-tanu kol b'-cho-rei-hem
הָרַגְתָּ וּבְכוֹרְךָ	You slew and Your firstborn	ha-rag-ta u-v'-cho-r'-cha
גָּאַלְתָּ וְיַם סוּף בָּקַעְתָּ	You redeemed. The Red Sea You split	ga-al-ta v'-yam suf ba-ka-ta
וְזֵדִים טִבַּעְתָּ	and the wicked You drowned.	v'-zei-dim ti-ba-ta
וִידִידִים הֶעֱבַרְתָּ	The beloved ones You brought through	vi-di-dim he-e-var-ta
וַיְכַסּוּ מַיִם צָרֵיהֶם	and the waters covered their enemies,	va-y'-cha-su ma-yim tza-rei-hem
אֶחָד מֵהֶם לֹא נוֹתָר	not one of them remained.	e-chad mei-hem lo notar
עַל זֹאת שִׁבְּחוּ אֲהוּבִים	Because of this the loved ones praised	al zot shi-b'-chu a-hu-vim
וְרוֹמְמוּ אֵל	and exalted God,	v'-ro-m'-mu El
וְנָתְנוּ יְדִידִים זְמִרוֹת	and the beloved ones offered hymns,	v'-na-t'-nu y'-di-dim z'-mirot
שִׁירוֹת וְתִשְׁבָּחוֹת	songs, and praises,	shi-rot v'-tish-bachot
בְּרָכוֹת וְהוֹדָאוֹת	blessings and thanksgivings	b'-ra-chot v' ho-da-ot
לְמֶלֶךְ אֵל חַי וְקַיָּם	to the King, God, living and enduring,	l'-melech El chai v'-ka-yam
רָם וְנִשָּׂא גָּדוֹל וְנוֹרָא	exalted and uplifted, great and awesome.	ram v'-ni-sa ga-dol v'-nora
מַשְׁפִּיל גֵּאִים	He humbles the haughty	mash-pil gei-im
וּמַגְבִּיהַּ שְׁפָלִים	and raises the lowly.	u-mag-bi-ha sh'-falim
מוֹצִיא אֲסִירִים	He brings out the captives	mo-tzi a-si-rim
וּפוֹדֶה עֲנָוִים	and frees the humble,	u-fo-deh a-na-vim
וְעוֹזֵר דַּלִּים	and helps the impoverished,	v'-ozer da-lim
וְעוֹנֶה לְעַמּוֹ בְּעֵת	and He answers His people when	v'-on-eh l'-amo b'-eit
שַׁוְּעָם אֵלָיו	they cry out to Him.	sha-v'-am ei-laiv
תְּהִלּוֹת לְאֵל עֶלְיוֹן	Praise to the Most High God!	t'-hi-lot l'-El El-yon
בָּרוּךְ הוּא וּמְבוֹרָךְ	Blessed is He and He is blessed.	Baruch hu u-m'-vo-rach

Shabbat Morning Service

בָּרוּךְ הוּא וּמְבוֹרָךְ	Blessed is He and He is blessed.	
	Baruch hu u-m'-vo-rach	
מֹשֶׁה וּבְנֵי יִשְׂרָאֵל	Moses and the children of Israel	
	Moshe u-v'-nei Yis-rael	
לְךָ עָנוּ שִׁירָה	raised a song to You	
	l'-cha anu shi-rah	
בְּשִׂמְחָה רַבָּה	with much joy,	
	b'-sim-cha ra-bah	
וְאָמְרוּ כֻלָּם:	and all of them proclaimed:	
	v'-am-ru chu-lam	

(congregation sings: first in Hebrew, then English)

Who is like unto Thee
O Lord, among the gods?
Who is like unto Thee,
Glorious in holiness!
Awesome in praises,
Doing wonders,
Who is like unto Thee!

מִי כָמֹכָה — **Who is like** You
mi cha-mo-chah
בָּאֵלִם יהוה — Adonai, among the gods!
ba-eilim Adonai
מִי כָּמֹכָה — Who is like You,
mi cha-mo-chah
נֶאְדָּר בַּקֹּדֶשׁ — glorious in holiness
ne-dar ba-kodesh
נוֹרָא תְהִלֹּת עֹשֵׂה פֶלֶא[1] — awesome in praises, doing wonders![1]
no-rah t'-hi-lot oseh fele

(Chazzan continues alone:)

שִׁירָה חֲדָשָׁה — With a new song
shi-ra cha-da-shah
שִׁבְּחוּ גְאוּלִים לְשִׁמְךָ — the redeemed praised Your Name
shi-b'-chu g'-u-lim l'-shim-cha
עַל שְׂפַת הַיָּם — at the seashore.
al s'-fat ha-yam
יַחַד כֻּלָּם הוֹדוּ — Together they all gave thanks
ya-chad ku-lam ho-du
וְהִמְלִיכוּ וְאָמְרוּ: — and affirmed Your kingship, and said:
v'-him-li-chu v'-am-ru

(congregation joins chazzan: first Hebrew then English)

יהוה יִמְלֹךְ לְעֹלָם וָעֶד:[2] — **Adonai will reign** forever and ever![2]
Adonai yim-loch l'-olam va-ed.

(Chazzan continues alone:)

צוּר יִשְׂרָאֵל — Rock of Israel
tzur Yisrael
קוּמָה בְּעֶזְרַת יִשְׂרָאֵל — arise to the aid of Israel
ku-mah b'-ez-rat Yis-rael
וּפְדֵה כִנְאֻמֶךָ — and liberate according to Your promise
u-f'-dei chin-u-mecha

(1) Ex 15:11 (2) Ex 15:18

Shabbat Morning Service 60

יְהוּדָה וְיִשְׂרָאֵל גֹּאֲלֵנוּ Judah and Israel. Our Redeemer—
Y'-hudah v'-Yis-ra-el go-a-leinu
יהוה צְבָאוֹת שְׁמוֹ Adonai of Hosts is His Name,
Adonai Tz'-va-ot sh'-mo
קְדוֹשׁ יִשְׂרָאֵל the Holy One of Israel.
k'-dosh Yis-rael
בָּרוּךְ אַתָּה יהוה Blessed are You Adonai
baruch ata Adonai
גָּאַל יִשְׂרָאֵל: Who redeemed Israel.
ga-al Yis-rael

שמונה עשרה **Shemonei Esrei** (The 18 Benedictions)
All Stand
(It is traditional to bend the knees at בָּרוּךְ, *baruch, to bow at* אַתָּה, *ata, and straighten at* יהוה, *Adonai)*
Chazzan begins alone

אֲדֹנָי שְׂפָתַי תִּפְתָּח Adonai, open my lips
Adonai s'-fa-tai tif-tach
וּפִי יַגִּיד תְּהִלָּתֶךָ:[1] and my mouth will declare Your praise.[1]
u-fi ya-gid t'-hi-la-techa

Congregation joins in

---

1. אבות 1. **COVENANT OF THE FATHERS**

בָּרוּךְ אַתָּה יהוה Blessed are You, Adonai
Baruch ata Adonai
אֱלֹהֵינוּ וֵאלֹהֵי אֲבוֹתֵינוּ our God, and God of our fathers;
Eloheinu vei-lo-hei a-vo-teinu
אֱלֹהֵי אַבְרָהָם אֱלֹהֵי God of Abraham, God of
Elohei Avraham Elohei
יִצְחָק וֵאלֹהֵי יַעֲקֹב Isaac, and God of Jacob;
Yitz-chak vei-lo-hei Ya-akov
הָאֵל הַגָּדוֹל הַגִּבּוֹר The great and mighty God,
ha-El ha-gadol ha-gi-bor
וְהַנּוֹרָא אֵל עֶלְיוֹן Who is awesome, God Most High
v'-ha-nora El El-yon
גּוֹמֵל חֲסָדִים טוֹבִים Who bestows good lovingkindness
go-meil cha-sa-dim tovim
וְקוֹנֵה הַכֹּל and is Owner of everything;
v'-konei ha-kol
וְזוֹכֵר חַסְדֵי אָבוֹת He remembers lovingkindness to the fathers
v'-zo-cheir chas-dei avot
וּמֵבִיא גוֹאֵל and brings a Redeemer
u-mei-vi go-eil

(1) Psalm 51:15

Shabbat Morning Service

לִבְנֵי בְנֵיהֶם to their children's children
liv-nei v'-nei-hem

לְמַעַן שְׁמוֹ בְּאַהֲבָה: for His own Name's sake in love.
l'-ma-an sh'-mo b'-a-havah

(between Yom Teruah [Rosh HaShanah] and Yom Kippur add)

זָכְרֵנוּ לְחַיִּים Remember us for life
za-ch'-reinu l'-cha-yim

מֶלֶךְ חָפֵץ בַּחַיִּים King Who desires life,
melech cha-feitz ba-cha-yim

כִּי נִכְתַּבְנוּ בְּסֵפֶר הַחַיִּים for we are written in the book of life
ki nich-tav-nu b'-sefer ha-cha-yim

לְמַעַן יֵשׁוּעַ מְשִׁיחֵנוּ on account of Yeshua our Messiah,
l'-ma-an Yeshua M'-shi-cheinu

אֱלֹהִים חַיִּים O living God.
Elohim cha-yim

מֶלֶךְ עוֹזֵר וּמוֹשִׁיעַ וּמָגֵן: King, Helper, Savior, and Shield;
melech ozeir u-mo-shi-a u-ma-gen

בָּרוּךְ אַתָּה יהוה Blessed are You, Adonai,
baruch ata Adonai

מָגֵן אַבְרָהָם: Shield of Abraham.
ma-gen Av-ra-ham

2. אתה גבור   2. GOD'S MIGHT

(Allow individuals to offer prayers for those sick and in need, then all pray together:)

אַתָּה גִבּוֹר לְעוֹלָם אֲדֹנָי **You are mighty forever,** my Master,
ata gi-bor l'-o-lam Adonai

מְחַיֶּה מֵתִים You resurrect the dead—
m'-cha-yeim mei-tim

אַתָּה רַב לְהוֹשִׁיעַ: You are mighty to save.
ata rav l'-ho-shi-a

(between Shemini Atzeret and Pesach add:)

מַשִּׁיב הָרוּחַ You make the wind blow
ma-shiv ha-ru-ach

וּמוֹרִיד הַגָּשֶׁם: and the rain to fall.
u-mo-rid ha-ga-shem

Shabbat Morning Service

מְכַלְכֵּל חַיִּים בְּחֶסֶד	You sustain the living in lovingkindness,	m'-chal-keil cha-yim b'-chesed
מְחַיֵּה מֵתִים	resurrecting the dead	m'-cha-yei mei-tim
בְּרַחֲמִים רַבִּים	with great compassion;	b'-ra-cha-mim ra-bim
סוֹמֵךְ נוֹפְלִים	Supporter of the fallen	so-meich no-f'-lim
וְרוֹפֵא חוֹלִים	and Healer of the sick;	v'-ro-fei cholim
וּמַתִּיר אֲסוּרִים	Releaser of the imprisoned	u-ma-tir a-su-rim
וּמְקַיֵּם אֱמוּנָתוֹ	and Fulfiller of His faithfulness	u-m'-ka-yeim e-mu-nato
לִישֵׁנֵי עָפָר	to those asleep in the dust.	li-shei-nei a-far
מִי כָמוֹךָ בַּעַל גְּבוּרוֹת	Who is like You, Master of wonders,	mi cha-mocha ba-al g'-vu-rot
וּמִי דּוֹמֶה לָּךְ	and Who compares to You,	u-mi do-meh lach
מֶלֶךְ מֵמִית	King Who causes death	melech mei-mit
וּמְחַיֶּה	and restores life,	u-m'-cha-yeh
וּמַצְמִיחַ יְשׁוּעָה:	and causes salvation to spring forth.	u-matz-mi-ach y'-shu-ah

(between Rosh Hashanah and Yom Kippur add)

מִי כָמוֹךָ אַב הָרַחֲמִים	Who is like You, merciful Father	mi-cha-mocha av ha-ra-cha-mim
זוֹכֵר יְצוּרָיו לְחַיִּים	Who remembers His creatures for life	zo-cheir y'-tzu-raiv l'-cha-yim
בְּרַחֲמִים	in mercy!	b'-ra-cha-mim

וְנֶאֱמָן אַתָּה	And You are faithful	v'-ne-e-man ata
לְהַחֲיוֹת מֵתִים	to restore life to the dead.	l'-ha-cha-yot mei-tim
בָּרוּךְ אַתָּה יהוה	Blessed are You, Adonai,	baruch ata Adonai
מְחַיֵּה הַמֵּתִים:	Resurrector of the dead.	m'-cha-yeih ha-mei-tim

קְדוּשָׁה Kedusha *(Holiness)*
(Chazzan together with the congregation:)

נְקַדֵּשׁ אֶת שִׁמְךָ בָּעוֹלָם **We will sanctify** Your Name in this world
n'-ka-deish et shim-cha ba-o-lam

כְּשֵׁם שֶׁמַּקְדִּישִׁים אוֹתוֹ just as they sanctify it
k'-shem she-mak-di-shim oto

בִּשְׁמֵי מָרוֹם כַּכָּתוּב עַל in heaven above, as it is written
bish-mei ma-rom ka-ka-tuv

יַד נְבִיאֶךָ: by the hand of Your prophet:
al yad n'-vi-e-cha

וְקָרָא זֶה אֶל זֶה וְאָמַר: "And he called one to the other and said:
v'-ka-ra zeh el zeh v'-amar

(Everyone sings, in Hebrew)

קָדוֹשׁ קָדוֹשׁ קָדוֹשׁ **Holy**, Holy, Holy
kadosh kadosh kadosh

יהוה צְבָאוֹת is Adonai of Hosts!
Adonai tz'-va-ot

מְלֹא כָל הָאָרֶץ כְּבוֹדוֹ[1] All the earth is full of His glory!"[1]
m'-lo chol ha-ar-etz k'-vo-do

(Chazzan alone:)

לְעֻמָּתָם בָּרוּךְ יֹאמֵרוּ: Those facing them say:
l'-u-ma-tam baruch yo-mei-ru

(Everyone: Hebrew then English)

בָּרוּךְ כְּבוֹד **Blessed** is the glory
baruch k'-vod

יהוה מִמְּקוֹמוֹ[2] of Adonai from His place.[2]
Adonai mi-m'-komo

(Chazzan alone:)

וּבְדִבְרֵי קָדְשְׁךָ And in Your holy words
u-v'-div-rei kod-sh'-cha

כָּתוּב לֵאמֹר: it is written:
ka-tuv lei-mor

(Everyone: Hebrew then English)

יִמְלֹךְ יהוה לְעוֹלָם **Adonai** will reign forever,
yim-loch Adonai l'-o-lam

אֱלֹהַיִךְ צִיּוֹן לְדֹר וָדֹר Your God, O Zion, in every generation.
Eloha-yich Tzi-yon l'-dor va-dor

הַלְלוּיָהּ[3] Halleluya![3]
ha-l'-lu-ya

(1) Is 6:3 (2) Ezek 3:12 (3) Psalm 146:10

Shabbat Morning Service

(Everyone sings in Hebrew)

לְדוֹר וָדוֹר **In all generations**
l'-dor va-dor

נַגִּיד גָּדְלֶךָ **we will declare Your greatness**
na-gid ga-d'-lecha

וּלְנֵצַח נְצָחִים **and to all eternity**
u-l'-nei-tzach n'-tza-chim

קְדֻשָּׁתְךָ נַקְדִּישׁ **we will sanctify Your holiness,**
k'-du-sha-t'cha nak-dish

וְשִׁבְחֲךָ אֱלֹהֵינוּ **and Your praise, our God,**
v'-shiv-cha-cha Eloheinu

מִפִּינוּ לֹא יָמוּשׁ **will not depart from our mouth**
mi-pinu lo ya-mush

לְעוֹלָם וָעֶד **forever and ever,**
l'-o-lam va-ed

(Chazzan alone)

כִּי אֵל מֶלֶךְ גָּדוֹל **because You are God, the Great King,**
ki El melech ga-dol

וְקָדוֹשׁ אָתָּה **and You are holy.**
v'-ka-dosh ata

(From Rosh HaShanah to Yom Kippur skip to shaded paragraph below)

בָּרוּךְ אַתָּה יהוה **Blessed are You, Adonai,**
baruch ata Adonai

הָאֵל הַקָּדוֹשׁ: **the Almighty, the Holy One.**
ha-El ha-ka-dosh

(*From Rosh HaShanah to Yom Kippur substitute this paragraph)

בָּרוּךְ אַתָּה יהוה **Blessed are You, Adonai,**
baruch ata Adonai

הַמֶּלֶךְ הַקָּדוֹשׁ **the King, the Holy One.**
ha-melech ha-ka-dosh

3. HOLINESS OF GOD'S NAME ‎3. קְדוּשַׁת הַשֵּׁם

Chazzan alone

אַתָּה קָדוֹשׁ וְשִׁמְךָ קָדוֹשׁ
You are holy and Your Name is holy
ata ka-dosh v'-shim-cha ka-dosh

וּקְדוֹשִׁים
and holy beings
u-k'-do-shim

בְּכָל יוֹם יְהַלְלוּךָ
praise You every day, forever.
b'-chol yom y'-ha-l'-lucha

*בָּרוּךְ אַתָּה יהוה
*Blessed are You, Adonai,
baruch ata Adonai

הָאֵל הַקָּדוֹשׁ:
the Almighty, the Holy One.
ha-El ha-ka-dosh

(*between Rosh HaShanah and Yom Kippur substitute:)

בָּרוּךְ אַתָּה יהוה
Blessed are You, Adonai,
baruch ata Adonai

הַמֶּלֶךְ הַקָּדוֹשׁ
the King, the Holy One.
ha-melech ha-ka-dosh

יִשְׂמַח מֹשֶׁה
Moses rejoiced
yis-mach Mo-sheh

בְּמַתְּנַת חֶלְקוֹ
in the gift of his portion,
b¯ma-t'-nat chel-ko

כִּי עֶבֶד נֶאֱמָן קָרָאתָ לּוֹ
that You called him a faithful servant.
ki eved ne-e-man ka-ra-ta lo

כְּלִיל תִּפְאֶרֶת
A crown of splendor
k'-lil tif-eret

בְּרֹאשׁוֹ נָתַתָּ בְּעָמְדוֹ
You placed on his head when he stood
b'-ro-sho na-ta-ta b'-am-do

לְפָנֶיךָ עַל הַר סִינַי
before You on Mount Sinai.
l'-fa-ne-cha al har Si-nai

וּשְׁנֵי לוּחוֹת אֲבָנִים הוֹרִיד
Two stone tablets he brought down
u-sh'-nei lu-chot a-va-nim ho-rid

בְּיָדוֹ וְכָתוּב בָּהֶם
in his hand, and written on them
b'-ya-do v'-cha-tuv ba-hem

שְׁמִירַת שַׁבָּת
was the observance of the Sabbath.
sh'-mi-rat sha-bat

וְכֵן כָּתוּב בְּתוֹרָתֶךָ:
And so it is written in Your Torah:
v'-chen ka-tuv b'-to-ra-techa

Chazzan and Congregation:

וְשָׁמְרוּ בְנֵי יִשְׂרָאֵל
And the children of Israel shall keep
v'-sha-m'-ru v'-nei Yis-ra-el

Shabbat Morning Service

אֶת הַשַּׁבָּת לַעֲשׂוֹת the Sabbath to make
et ha-sha-bat la-a-sot

אֶת הַשַּׁבָּת the Sabbath
et ha-sha-bat

לְדֹרֹתָם throughout their generations
l'-do-ro-tam

בְּרִית עוֹלָם בֵּינִי an eternal covenant. Between Me and
b'-rit o-lam bei-ni u-vein

וּבֵין בְּנֵי יִשְׂרָאֵל אוֹת הִיא between the children of Israel it is a sign
b'-nei Yis-ra-el ot hi

לְעֹלָם כִּי שֵׁשֶׁת יָמִים forever, that in six days
l'-o-lam ki shei-shet ya-mim

עָשָׂה יְהוָה אֶת הַשָּׁמַיִם Adonai made the heavens
a-sah Adonai et ha-sha-ma-im

וְאֶת הָאָרֶץ and the earth,
v'-et ha-aretz

וּבַיּוֹם הַשְּׁבִיעִי שָׁבַת and on the seventh day He rested
u-va-yom ha-sh'-vi-i sha-bat

וַיִּנָּפַשׁ[1] and was refreshed.[1]
va-yi-na-fash

Chazzan continues alone:

אֱלֹהֵינוּ וֵאלֹהֵי אֲבוֹתֵינוּ Our God and God of our fathers,
Eloheinu vei-lo-hei a-vo-tei-nu

רְצֵה נָא בִמְנוּחָתֵנוּ may You be pleased with our rest.
r'-tzei na vim-nu-cha-teinu

קַדְּשֵׁנוּ בְּמִצְוֹתֶיךָ Sanctify us in Your commandments
ka-d'-sheinu b'-mitz-vo-techa

וְתֵן חֶלְקֵנוּ בְּתוֹרָתֶךָ and grant our share in Your Torah;
v'-tein chel-keinu b'-to-ra-techa

שַׂבְּעֵנוּ מִטּוּבֶךָ satisfy us with Your goodness
sa-b'-einu mi-tu-vecha

וְשַׂמְּחֵנוּ and cause us to rejoice
v'-sa-m'-cheinu

בִּישׁוּעָתֶךָ וְטַהֵר לִבֵּנוּ in Your salvation and purify our heart
bi-shu-a-techa v'-ta-heir li-beinu

לְעָבְדְּךָ בֶּאֱמֶת to serve You in truth.
l'-av-d'-cha be-emet

וְהַנְחִילֵנוּ יְהוָה אֱלֹהֵינוּ Adonai our God, cause us to inherit
v'-han-chi-leinu Adonai Eloheinu

בְּאַהֲבָה וּבְרָצוֹן in love and truth
b'-a-ha-vah u-v'-ra-tzon

שַׁבַּת קָדְשֶׁךָ Your holy Sabbath,
sha-bat kod-she-cha

(1) Ex 31:16-17

Shabbat Morning Service

וְיָנוּחוּ בוֹ כָּל יִשְׂרָאֵל and may they rest in it, all of Israel,
v'-ya-nu-chu vo kol Yis-ra-el

מְקַדְּשֵׁי שְׁמֶךָ those who sanctify Your Name.
m'-ka-d'-shei sh'-me-cha

בָּרוּךְ אַתָּה יהוה Blessed are You, Adonai,
baruch ata Adonai

מְקַדֵּשׁ הַשַּׁבָּת: Who sanctifies the Sabbath.
m'-ka-deish ha-sha-bat

---

17. עבודה / 17. DIVINE SERVICE

Chazzan continues alone:

רְצֵה יהוה אֱלֹהֵינוּ Be pleased, Adonai our God,
r'-tzei Adonai Eloheinu

בְּעַמְּךָ יִשְׂרָאֵל with Your people Israel
b'-a-m'cha Yis-ra-el

וּבִתְפִלָּתָם and their prayers,
u-vit-fi-la-tam

וְהָשֵׁב אֶת הָעֲבוֹדָה and return the service
v'-ha-sheiv et ha-a-vo-dah

לִדְבִיר to the Most Holy Place
lid-vir

בֵּיתֶךָ in Your abode
vei-techa

וְאִשֵּׁי יִשְׂרָאֵל and the fire offerings of Israel;
v'-i-shei Yis-ra-el

וּתְפִלָּתָם בְּאַהֲבָה תְקַבֵּל and accept their prayer lovingly
u-t'-fi-la-tam b'-a-ha-vah t'-ka-beil

בְּרָצוֹן and willingly.
b'-ra-tzon

וּתְהִי לְרָצוֹן תָּמִיד And may You constantly be pleased
u-t'-hi l'-ra-tzon ta-mid

עֲבוֹדַת יִשְׂרָאֵל with the service of Israel
a-vo-dat Yis-ra-el

עַמֶּךָ Your people.
a-me-cha

(*On Rosh Chodesh and Chol HaMoed, the following prayer is added*)

אֱלֹהֵינוּ וֵאלֹהֵי אֲבוֹתֵינוּ Our God and God of our fathers,
Eloheinu vei-lohei a-vo-tei-nu

יַעֲלֶה וְיָבֹא וְיַגִּיעַ may there ascend, come, and reach,
ya-a-leh v'-ya-vo v'-ya-gi-a

וְיֵרָאֶה וְיֵרָצֶה וְיִשָּׁמַע appear, be desired, and heard
v'-yei-ra-eh v'-yei-ra-tzeh v'-yi-sha-ma

Shabbat Morning Service

וְיִפָּקֵד וְיִזָּכֵר	counted and recalled
	v'-yi-pa-keid v'-yi-za-cheir
זִכְרוֹנֵנוּ וּפִקְדוֹנֵנוּ	our rememberance and reckoning
	zich-ro-nei-nu u-fik-do-nei-nu
וְזִכְרוֹן	and the rememberance of
	v'-zich-ron
אֲבוֹתֵינוּ	our fathers,
	a-vo-tei-nu
וְזִכְרוֹן	the rememberance of
	v'-zich-ron
יֵשׁוּעַ הַמָּשִׁיחַ	Yeshua the Messiah
	Ye-shu-a Ha-Ma-shi-ach
בֶּן דָּוִד עַבְדֶּךָ	son of David, Your Servant
	ben Da-vid av-de-cha
וְזִכְרוֹן יְרוּשָׁלַיִם	the rememberance of Jerusalem
	v'-zich-ron Y'-ru-sha-la-yim
עִיר קָדְשֶׁךָ	the city of Your sanctuary,
	ir kod-she-cha
וְזִכְרוֹן כָּל	and the rememberance of all
	v'-zich-ron kol
עַמְּךָ בֵּית יִשְׂרָאֵל	Your people the house of Israel
	a-m'-cha beit Yis-ra-el
לְפָנֶיךָ לִפְלֵיטָה	before You, for survival
	l'-fa-ne-cha lif-lei-tah
לְטוֹבָה	for well-being,
	l'-to-vah
לְחֵן וּלְחֶסֶד	for grace, lovingkindness
	l'-chen u-l'-che-sed
וּלְרַחֲמִים	and compassion,
	u-l'-ra-cha-mim
לְחַיִּים וּלְשָׁלוֹם	for life and peace,
	l'-cha-yim u-l'-sha-lom
בְּיוֹם	on this day of
	b'-yom
רֹאשׁ הַחֹדֶשׁ הַזֶּה	Rosh Chodesh
	rosh ha-cho-desh ha-zeh
חַג הַמַּצּוֹת הַזֶּה	the Festival of Unleavened Bread
	chag ha-ma-tzot ha-zeh
חַג הַסֻּכּוֹת הַזֶּה	the Festival of Sukkot
	chag ha-su-kot ha-zeh

Shabbat Morning Service

זָכְרֵנוּ יהוה אֱלֹהֵינוּ	Remember us, Adonai our God
	za-ch'-rei-nu Adonai Eloheinu
בּוֹ לְטוֹבָה	on this day for well-being,
	bo l'-to-vah
וּפָקְדֵנוּ בוֹ לִבְרָכָה	and visit us on it for a blessing.
	u-fak-dei-nu bo liv-ra-chah
וְהוֹשִׁיעֵנוּ בוֹ לְחַיִּים	Deliver us on it for life,
	v'-ho-shi-ei-nu vo l'-cha-yim
וּבִדְבַר יְשׁוּעָה	By Your word of salvation
	u-vid-var y'-shu-ah
וְרַחֲמִים	and compassion,
	v'-ra-cha-mim
חוּס וְחָנֵּנוּ	spare us and show us grace
	chus v'-cha-nei-nu
וְרַחֵם עָלֵינוּ	and have compassion on us
	v'-ra-chem a-lei-nu
וְהוֹשִׁיעֵנוּ	and save us,
	v'-ho-shi-ei-nu
כִּי אֵלֶיךָ עֵינֵינוּ	for our eyes are directed to You,
	ki ei-lecha ei-nei-nu
כִּי אֵל	because You are God,
	ki El
מֶלֶךְ חַנּוּן	King, Gracious,
	me-lech cha-nun
וְרַחוּם אָתָּה	and Compassionate.
	v'-ra-chum ata

וְתֶחֱזֶינָה עֵינֵינוּ	And may our eyes behold
	v'-te-che-zei-nah ei-nei-nu
בְּשׁוּבְךָ לְצִיּוֹן	Your return to Zion
	b'-shu-v'-cha l'-Tzi-yon
בְּרַחֲמִים	in compassion.
	b'-ra-cha-mim
בָּרוּךְ אַתָּה יהוה	Blessed are You, Adonai,
	baruch ata Adonai
הַמַּחֲזִיר שְׁכִינָתוֹ	Who returns His Divine Presence
	ha-ma-cha-zir sh'-ki-na-to
לְצִיּוֹן	to Zion.
	l'-Tzi-yon

Shabbat Morning Service 70

18. מודים אנחנו | 18. WE ARE THANKFUL

(Give individuals opportunity to share God's blessings in their lives, then all pray together:)

מוֹדִים אֲנַחְנוּ לָךְ	We are thankful to You	mo-dim a-nachnu lach
שָׁאַתָּה הוּא יהוה אֱלֹהֵינוּ	that You are Adonai our God,	sha-a-tah hu Adonai Eloheinu
וֵאלֹהֵי אֲבוֹתֵינוּ	and the God of our fathers	vei-lohei a-vo-teinu
לְעוֹלָם וָעֶד צוּר חַיֵּינוּ	for all eternity. Rock of our lives,	l'-o-lam va-ed tzur cha-yeinu
מָגֵן יִשְׁעֵנוּ אַתָּה הוּא	Shield of our salvation are You	ma-gein yish-einu ata hu
לְדוֹר וָדוֹר	from generation to generation.	l'-dor va-dor
נוֹדֶה לְּךָ	We give thanks to You	no-deh l'-cha
וּנְסַפֵּר תְּהִלָּתֶךָ	and recount Your praise	u-n'-sa-peir t'-hi-la-techa
עַל חַיֵּינוּ הַמְּסוּרִים	for our lives which are committed	al cha-yeinu ha-m'-su-rim
בְּיָדֶךָ וְעַל נִשְׁמוֹתֵינוּ	into Your hand, and for our souls	b'-ya-decha v'-al nish-mo-teinu
הַפְּקוּדוֹת לָךְ	which are entrusted to You,	ha-p'-ku-dot lach
וְעַל נִסֶּיךָ	and for Your miracles	v'-al ni-seicha
שֶׁבְּכָל יוֹם עִמָּנוּ	that are with us every day	she-b'-chol yom i-manu
וְעַל נִפְלְאוֹתֶיךָ	and for Your wonders	v'-al nif-l'-o-teicha
וְטוֹבוֹתֶיךָ שֶׁבְּכָל עֵת	and Your goodness at all times—	v'-to-vo-teicha she-b'-chol eit
עֶרֶב וָבֹקֶר וְצָהֳרָיִם	evening, morning, and afternoon.	erev va-vo-ker v'-tza-ho-ra-im
הַטּוֹב	You are good,	ha-tov
כִּי לֹא כָלוּ רַחֲמֶיךָ	for Your compassion is never exhausted,	ki lo cha-lu ra-cha-meicha
וְהַמְרַחֵם	and You are compassionate,	v'-ham-ra-cheim
כִּי לֹא תַמּוּ חֲסָדֶיךָ	for Your lovingkindness never ceases.	ki lo ta-mu cha-sa-deicha mei-olam

Shabbat Morning Service

מֵעוֹלָם קִוִּינוּ לָךְ
Forever we have hoped in You!
ki-vinu lach

וְעַל כֻּלָּם יִתְבָּרַךְ
And for all the foregoing blessed
v'-al ku-lam yit-ba-rach

וְיִתְרוֹמַם שִׁמְךָ מַלְכֵּנוּ
and exalted be Your Name, our King,
v'-yit-ro-mam shim-cha mal-keinu

תָּמִיד לְעוֹלָם וָעֶד
constantly, for all eternity.
ta-mid l'-olam va-ed

(Between Yom Teruah [Rosh HaShanah] and Yom Kippur add:)

וּכְתוֹב לְחַיִּים טוֹבִים
Inscribe for a good life
u-k'-tov l'-cha-yim to-vim

כָּל בְּנֵי בְרִיתֶךָ
all who are children of Your covenant.
kol b'-nei v'-ri-techa

וְכֹל הַחַיִּים יוֹדוּךָ[1]
And all the living shall thank You[1]
v'-chol ha-cha-yim yo-du-cha

וִיהַלְלוּ אֶת שִׁמְךָ
and praise Your Name
vi-ha-l'-lu et shim-cha

בֶּאֱמֶת הָאֵל יְשׁוּעָתֵנוּ[2]
in truth. The Almighty, our salvation,[2]
be-emet ha-El y'-shu-a-teinu

וְעֶזְרָתֵנוּ
and our help.
v'-ez-ra-teinu

בָּרוּךְ אַתָּה יהוה
Blessed are You, Adonai.
baruch ata Adonai

הַטּוֹב שִׁמְךָ
"The Beneficent" is Your Name
ha-tov shim-cha

וּלְךָ נָאֶה לְהוֹדוֹת
and to You it is fitting to give praise.
u-l'-cha na-eh l'-ho-dot.

19. שלום   19. PEACE

(follow Chazzan's instructions for reciting "Grant Peace")

שִׂים שָׁלוֹם טוֹבָה וּבְרָכָה
Grant peace, goodness and blessing,
sim shalom to-vah u-v'-ra-cha

חֵן וָחֶסֶד וְרַחֲמִים
grace, lovingkindness and compassion
chen va-chesed v'-ra-cha-mim

עָלֵינוּ וְעַל כָּל
upon us and upon all
a-leinu v'-al kol

יִשְׂרָאֵל עַמֶּךָ
Israel Your people.
Yis-ra-el a-mecha

(1) Ps 44:8 (2) Ps 68:20[19]

Shabbat Morning Service

בָּרְכֵנוּ אָבִינוּ כֻּלָּנוּ כְּאֶחָד	Bless us, our Father, all of us as one
	ba-r'-cheinu a-vinu ku-lanu k'-echad
בְּאוֹר פָּנֶיךָ	with the light of Your face
	b'-or pa-necha
כִּי בְאוֹר פָּנֶיךָ	because by the light of Your face
	ki v'-or pa-necha
נָתַתָּ לָּנוּ יהוה אֱלֹהֵינוּ	You gave to us, Adonai our God,
	na-ta-ta lanu Adonai Eloheinu
תּוֹרַת חַיִּים וְאַהֲבַת	a Torah of life and the love of
	torat cha-yim v'-a-ha-vat
חֶסֶד וּצְדָקָה וּבְרָכָה	kindness, righteousness, blessing,
	chesed u-tz'-da-kah u-v'-ra-chah
וְרַחֲמִים וְחַיִּים וְשָׁלוֹם	compassion, life, and peace.
	v'-ra-cha-mim v'-cha-yim v'-shalom
וְטוֹב בְּעֵינֶיךָ	So may it be good in Your eyes
	v'-tov b'-ei-necha
לְבָרֵךְ אֶת עַמְּךָ יִשְׂרָאֵל	to bless Your people Israel
	l'-va-reich et a-m'–cha Yis-ra-el
בְּכָל עֵת וּבְכָל שָׁעָה	at all times and in every hour
	b'-chol eit u-v'-chol sha-ah
בִּשְׁלוֹמֶךָ	with Your peace.
	bish-lo-mecha

(Between Yom Teruah [Rosh HaShanah] and Yom Kippur add:)

בְּסֵפֶר חַיִּים בְּרָכָה	In the book of life, blessing,
	b'-sei-fer cha-yim b'-ra-chah
וְשָׁלוֹם וּפַרְנָסָה טוֹבָה	peace, and abundant maintenance
	v'-sha-lom u-far-na-sah to-vah
נִזָּכֵן וְנִכָּתֵב לְפָנֶיךָ	may we be remembered and written
	ni-za-chein v'-ni-ka-teiv l'-fa-necha
לְמַעַן יֵשׁוּעַ מְשִׁיחֵנוּ	for the sake of Yeshua our Messiah
	l'-ma-an Yeshua m'-shi-cheinu
אֲנַחְנוּ וְכָל עַמְּךָ	we and all Your people,
	a-nachnu v'-chol a-m'-cha
בֵּית יִשְׂרָאֵל	the house of Israel,
	beit Yis-ra-el
לְחַיִּים טוֹבִים וּלְשָׁלוֹם	for a good life and for peace.
	l'-cha-yim to-vim u-l'-shalom

בָּרוּךְ אַתָּה יהוה	Blessed are You, Adonai,
	baruch ata Adonai
הַמְבָרֵךְ אֶת עַמּוֹ	Who blesses His people
	ham-va-reich et amo
יִשְׂרָאֵל בַּשָּׁלוֹם	Israel with peace.
	Yis-ra-el ba-shalom

Shabbat Morning Service

(Chazzan continues alone:)

יְהִי רָצוֹן מִלְּפָנֶיךָ	May it be Your will,	*y'-hi ra-tzon mil-fa-necha*
יהוה אֱלֹהֵינוּ וֵאלֹהֵי	Adonai our God and God of	*Adonai Eloheinu vei-lo-hei*
אֲבוֹתֵינוּ	our fathers,	*a-vo-teinu*
שֶׁיִּבָּנֶה בֵּית הַמִּקְדָּשׁ	that the Holy Temple be rebuilt	*she-yi-ba-neh beit ha-mik-dash*
בִּמְהֵרָה בְיָמֵינוּ	quickly, in our days;	*bim-hei-rah v'-ya-meinu*
וְתֵן חֶלְקֵנוּ בְּתוֹרָתֶךָ	and grant our portion in Your Torah	*v'-tein chel-keinu b'-to-ra-techa*
וְשָׁם נַעֲבָדְךָ בְּיִרְאָה	and there let us serve You in reverence	*v'-sham na-a-va-d'-cha b'-yir-ah*
כִּימֵי עוֹלָם	as in days of old	*ki-mei o-lam*
וּכְשָׁנִים קַדְמוֹנִיּוֹת	and in earlier years.	*u-ch'-sha-nim kad-mo-ni-yot*
וְעָרְבָה לַיהוה	And may it be pleasing to Adonai,	*v'-a-r'-vah la-donai*
מִנְחַת יְהוּדָה וִירוּשָׁלָיִם	the offering of Judah and Jerusalem	*min-chat Y'-hudah vi-ru-sha-la-im*
כִּימֵי עוֹלָם	as in days of old	*ki-mei o-lam*
וּכְשָׁנִים קַדְמוֹנִיּוֹת	and in earlier years.	*u-k'-sha-nim kad-mo-ni-yot*

Shabbat Morning Service

(Chazzan may select from the following passages for the congregation to recite)

כִּי יְהִי לְבַבְכֶם Let This Thinking Be in You

The confession written by Paul in Philippians 2:5-8 was a well known confession used by early followers of Yeshua to acknowledge Him as Messiah, and as the Savior of mankind.

כִּי יְהִי לְבַבְכֶם **Let this** thinking be in you,
ki y'-hi l'-vav-chem

כִּלְבַב הַמָּשִׁיחַ יֵשׁוּעַ: as it was in Yeshua the Messiah,
kil-vav ha-Ma-shi-ach Ye-shu-a

אֲשֶׁר אַף כִּי־הָיָה Who being in the very
a-sher af ki ha-yah

בִּדְמוּת הָאֱלֹהִים nature of God
bid-mut ha-Elohim

לֹא־חָשַׁב לוֹ לְשָׁלָל did not think it necessary to retain
lo cha-shav lo l'-sha-lal

הֱיוֹתוֹ שָׁוֶה לֵאלֹהִים: His position with God.
he-yo-to sha-veh lei-lo-him

כִּי אִם־הִפְשִׁיט אֶת־עַצְמוֹ But He emptied Himself,
ki im hif-shit et atz-mo

וַיִּלְבַּשׁ and clothed Himself
va-yil-bash

דְּמוּת עֶבֶד in the likeness of a servant,
d'-mut e-ved

וַיְהִי דוֹמֶה לִבְנֵי אָדָם and came in the image of mankind.
va-y'-hi do-meh liv-nei a-dam

וַיִּמָּצֵא בִתְכוּנָתוֹ And being found in appearance
va-yi-ma-tzei vit-chu-na-to

כְּבֶן אָדָם: וַיִּשָּׁפֵל as a man, He humbled
k'-ven a-dam va-yash-peil

אֶת־נַפְשׁוֹ וַיִּכָּנַע עַד־מָוֶת Himself and became obedient to death,
et naf-sho va-yi-ka-na ad ma-vet

עַד־מִיתַת הַצְּלִיבָה: even death on an execution stake.
ad mi-tat ha-tz'-li-vah

עַל־כֵּן הִגְבִּיהוּ הָאֱלֹהִים Therefore God exalted Him
al ken hig-bi-ho ha-Elohim

מְאֹד וַיִּתֶּן־לוֹ שֵׁם exceedingly, bestowing on Him a Name
m'-od va-yi-tein lo shem

נַעֲלֶה עַל־כָּל־שֵׁם: which is above all names,
na-a-leh al kol shem

אֲשֶׁר בְּשֵׁם יֵשׁוּעַ that at the Name of Yeshua
a-sher b'-shem Ye-shu-a

תִּכְרַע כָּל־בֶּרֶךְ every knee will bow
tich-ra kol berech

74

אֲשֶׁר בַּשָּׁמַיִם וּבָאָרֶץ whether in heaven or on the earth
a-sher ba-sha-ma-im u-va-aretz

וּמִתַּחַת לָאָרֶץ: or under the earth.
u-mi-ta-chat la-aretz

וְכָל־לָשׁוֹן תּוֹדֶה And every tongue will acknowledge
v'-chol la-shon to-deh

כִּי אָדוֹן יֵשׁוּעַ הַמָּשִׁיחַ that Yeshua the Messiah is Master
ki a-don Ye-shu-a ha-Ma-shi-ach

לִכְבוֹד אֱלֹהִים הָאָב: to the glory of God the Father.
lich-vod Elohim ha-av

גדול סוד Great Is the Mystery

Taken from 1 Timothy 3:16, this short, poetic confession encapsulates the incarnation of Yeshua

וּבְוַדַּי גָּדוֹל סוֹד **Without** dispute great is the mystery
u-v'-va-dai ga-dol sod

הַחֲסִידוּת of godliness:
ha-cha-si-dut

אֲשֶׁר נִגְלָה בַבָּשָׂר He Who was revealed in the flesh,
a-sher nig-lah va-ba-sar

נִצְדַּק בָּרוּחַ was vindicated by the Spirit,
nitz-dak ba-ru-ach

נִרְאָה לַמַּלְאָכִים beheld by angels,
nir-ah la-mal-a-chim

הֻגַּד בַּגּוֹיִם proclaimed among the nations,
hu-gad ba-go-im

נִתְקַבֵּל בֶּאֱמוּנָה בָּעוֹלָם received by faith in the world,
nit-ka-beil be-e-mu-nah ba-olam

נַעֲלָה בְּכָבוֹד: taken up in glory.
na-a-lah b'-cha-vod

חסד אלהים The Grace of God
(Titus 2:11-14)

כִּי הוֹפִיעַ חֶסֶד אֱלֹהִים **For** the grace of God has appeared
ki ho-fi-a che-sed Elohim

לְהוֹשִׁיעַ אֶת־כָּל־בְּנֵי bringing salvation to all people,
l'-ho-shi-a et kol b'-nei ha-a-dam

הָאָדָם: וּלְהַדְרִיךְ אֹתָנוּ teaching us
u-l'-had-rich o-ta-nu

לְמַעַן נְתַעֵב to say "No!" to
l'-ma-an n'-ta-eiv

Shabbat Morning Service

הָרֶשַׁע וְתַאֲוֹת הָעוֹלָם	wickedness and worldly passions	*ha-re-sha v'-ta-a-ot ha-o-lam*
וְנִתְהַלֵּךְ בָּעוֹלָם הַזֶּה	and to walk in this present age	*v'-nit-ha-leich ba-olam ha-zeh*
בִּצְנִיעוּת וּבְצֶדֶק	with self-control, righteousness	*bitz-ni-ut u-v'-tzedek*
וּבַחֲסִידוּת	and godliness;	*u-va-cha-si-dut*
וּנְחַכֶּה	and that we constantly await	*u-n'-cha-keh*
לַתִּקְוָה הַמְאֻשֶּׁרֶת	the blessed hope	*la-tik-vah ham-a-she-ret*
וּלְהוֹפָעַת כְּבוֹד	and glorious appearing of	*u-l'-ho-fa-at k'-vod*
אֱלֹהֵינוּ הַגָּדוֹל	our great God	*Eloheinu ha-ga-dol*
וּמוֹשִׁיעֵנוּ	and our Savior,	*u-mo-shi-einu*
יֵשׁוּעַ הַמָּשִׁיחַ	Yeshua the Messiah	*Ye-shu-a ha-Ma-shi-ach*
אֲשֶׁר־נָתַן אֶת־נַפְשׁוֹ	Who gave His life	*a-sher na-tan et naf-sho*
בַּעֲדֵנוּ לִפְדוֹת אֹתָנוּ	for us to redeem us	*ba-a-dei-nu lif-dot o-tanu*
מִכָּל־עָוֶל	from every transgression	*mi-kol a-vel*
וּלְטַהֵר לוֹ	and to purify for Himself	*u-l'-ta-heir lo*
עַם סְגֻלָּה	a treasured people,	*am s'-gu-lah*
הַזָּרִיז בְּמַעֲשִׂים טוֹבִים	eager to do good deeds.	*ha-za-riz b'-ma-a-sim to-vim*

תפילת התלמידים The Disciples' Prayer
(Matthew 6:9-14)

אָבִינוּ שֶׁבַּשָּׁמַיִם	**Our Father** Who is in heaven	*a-vi-nu she-ba-sha-ma-yim*
יִתְקַדֵּשׁ שִׁמְךָ	may Your Name be sanctified.	*yit-ka-deish shim-cha*
תָּבוֹא מַלְכוּתְךָ	May Your kingdom come,	*ta-vo mal-chu-t'-cah*
יֵעָשֶׂה רְצוֹנְךָ	Your will be done	*yei-a-seh r'-tzo-n'-cha*
כְּבַשָּׁמַיִם כֵּן בָּאָרֶץ	on earth as it is in heaven.	*k'-va-sha-ma-yim ken ba-aretz*

אֶת לֶחֶם חֻקֵּנוּ	The bread we need	et le-chem chu-kei-nu
תֵּן לָנוּ הַיּוֹם	give to us today,	tein lanu ha-yom
וּסְלַח לָנוּ עַל חֲטָאֵינוּ	and forgive us our sins	u-s'-lach lanu al cha-ta-ei-nu
כְּפִי שֶׁסּוֹלְחִים גַּם אֲנַחְנוּ	just as we also forgive	k'-fi she-so-l'-chim gam a-nach-nu
לַחוֹטְאִים לָנוּ	those who sin against us.	la-cho-t'-im la-nu
וְאַל תְּבִיאֵנוּ לִידֵי נִסָּיוֹן	And lead us not into temptation	v'-al t'-vi-einu li-dei ni-sa-yon
כִּי אִם חַלְּצֵנוּ מִן הָרָע	but deliver us from evil;	ki im cha-l'-tzei-nu min ha-ra
כִּי לְךָ הַמַּמְלָכָה	For to You belongs the kingdom	ki l'-cha ha-mam-la-chah
וְהַגְּבוּרָה וְהַתִּפְאֶרֶת	and the power and the glory	v'-ha-g'-vu-rah v'-ha-tif-e-ret
לְעוֹלְמֵי עוֹלָמִים אָמֵן	for all eternity. Amein.	l'-o-l'-mei o-la-mim amein

Torah Service

קריאת התורה Reading of the Torah

(Chazzan and congregation recite together:)

אֵין כָּמוֹךָ	**There is none** like You	ein ka-mo-cha
בָּאֱלֹהִים יהוה	among the gods, Adonai	va-ei-lo-him Adonai
וְאֵין כְּמַעֲשֶׂיךָ	and there is nothing like Your works.	v'-ein k'-ma-a-se-cha
מַלְכוּתְךָ מַלְכוּת	Your kingship is the kingship	mal-chu-t'-cha mal-chut
כָּל עוֹלָמִים	for all eternities,	kol o-la-mim
וּמֶמְשַׁלְתְּךָ בְּכָל	and Your rule is throughout every	u-mem-shal-t'-cha b'-chol
דֹּר וָדֹר	generation.	dor va-dor

Shabbat Morning Service **78**

(Chazzan and Congregation: Hebrew, then English)

יהוה מֶלֶךְ יהוה מָלָךְ **Adonai is King**, Adonai was King,
Adonai me-lech Adonai ma-lach
יהוה יִמְלֹךְ לְעֹלָם וָעֶד Adonai will be King forever and ever.
Adonai yim-loch l'-olam va-ed
יהוה עֹז לְעַמּוֹ יִתֵּן Adonai will give strength to His people.
Adonai oz l'-amo yi-ten
יהוה יְבָרֵךְ אֶת עַמּוֹ Adonai will bless His people
Adonai y'-va-reich et a-mo
בַּשָּׁלוֹם with peace.
va-sha-lom

(Chazzan alone)

אַב הָרַחֲמִים Father of compassion
av ha-ra-cha-mim
הֵיטִיבָה בִרְצוֹנְךָ Do good, according to Your will,
hei-ti-vah vir-tzo-n'-cha
אֶת צִיּוֹן to Zion.
et Tzi-yon
תִּבְנֶה חוֹמוֹת May You rebuild the walls of
tiv-neh cho-mot
יְרוּשָׁלָיִם Jerusalem.
Y'-ru-sha-la-yim
כִּי בְךָ לְבַד בָּטָחְנוּ For in You alone do we trust,
ki v'-cha l'-vad ba-tach-nu
מֶלֶךְ אֵל King, Almighty,
me-lech El
רָם וְנִשָּׂא Exalted and Uplifted One,
ram v'-ni-sa
אֲדוֹן עוֹלָמִים Master of the worlds.
a-don ol-la-mim

*(Designated person opens the Ark:
then the congregation stands and Chazzan and Congregation recite:)*

וַיְהִי בִּנְסֹעַ הָאָרֹן **Whenever the Ark** traveled,
va-y'-hi bin-so-a ha-a-ron
וַיֹּאמֶר מֹשֶׁה Moses would say,
va-yo-mer Mo-she
קוּמָה יהוה Arise, Adonai
kuma Adonai
וְיָפֻצוּ אֹיְבֶיךָ and let Your enemies be scattered
v'-ya-fu-tzu o-y'-ve-cha
וְיָנֻסוּ מְשַׂנְאֶיךָ and let those who hate You flee
v'-ya-nu-su m'-san-e-cha

(1) Num 10:35

Shabbat Morning Service

מִפָּנֶיךָ:[1]
from before You.[1]
mi-pa-nei-cha

כִּי מִצִּיּוֹן תֵּצֵא תוֹרָה
For from Zion will go forth the Torah
ki mi-Tzi-yon tei-tzei torah

וּדְבַר יהוה מִירוּשָׁלָיִם:[2]
and the word of Adonai from Jerusalem![2]
u-d'-var Adonai mi-ru-sha-la-yim

בָּרוּךְ שֶׁנָּתַן תּוֹרָה
Blessed is He Who gave the Torah
baruch she-na-tan torah

לְעַמּוֹ יִשְׂרָאֵל
to His people, Israel
l'-amo Yis-ra-el

בִּקְדֻשָּׁתוֹ:
in His holiness.
bik-du-sha-to

Chazzan and Congregation recite in Hebrew then English:

שְׁמַע יִשְׂרָאֵל
Hear, O Israel,
Shema Yisrael

יהוה אֱלֹהֵינוּ יהוה אֶחָד
Adonai is our God, Adonai is one!
Adonai Eloheinu Adonai echad

אֶחָד אֱלֹהֵינוּ
Our God is One
echad Eloheinu

גָּדוֹל אֲדוֹנֵינוּ
Great is our Master,
gadol Adoneinu

קָדוֹשׁ שְׁמוֹ
Holy is His Name!
kadosh sh'-mo

Chazzan alone:

גַּדְּלוּ לַיהוה אִתִּי
Magnify Adonai with me
ga-d'-lu la-Adonai i-ti

וּנְרוֹמְמָה שְׁמוֹ יַחְדָּו:[3]
and let us exalt His Name together.[3]
u-n'-ro-m'-mah sh'-mo yach-dav

The Congregation responds:

לְךָ יהוה הַגְּדֻלָּה
The greatness belongs to You, Adonai,
l'-cha Adonai ha-g'-du-lah

וְהַגְּבוּרָה וְהַתִּפְאֶרֶת
and the power, the glory,
v'-ha-g'-vu-rah v'-ha-tif-eret

וְהַנֵּצַח וְהַהוֹד
the victory, and the beauty;
v'-ha-nei-tzach v'-ha-hod

כִּי כֹל בַּשָּׁמַיִם וּבָאָרֶץ
everything in heaven and on earth
ki-chol ba-sha-ma-yim u-va-a-retz

לְךָ:
is Yours—
l'-cha

יהוה הַמַּמְלָכָה
Yours, Adonai is the kingdom
Adonai ha-mam-la-chah

(1) Num 10:35 (2) Is 2:3, cf. Mic 4:2 (3) Ps 34:3[4]

Shabbat Morning Service **80**

וְהַמִּתְנַשֵּׂא לְכֹל לְרֹאשׁ:	and You are sovereign over every leader.
	v'-ha-mit-na-sei l'-chol l'-rosh
רוֹמְמוּ יהוה אֱלֹהֵינוּ	Exalt Adonai our God
	ro-m'-mu Adonai Eloheinu
וְהִשְׁתַּחֲווּ לַהֲדֹם רַגְלָיו	and worship at His footstool
	v'-hish-ta-cha-vu la-ha-dom rag-laiv
קָדוֹשׁ הוּא:[1]	Holy is He.[1]
	ka-dosh hu
רוֹמְמוּ יהוה אֱלֹהֵינוּ	Exalt Adonai our God
	ro-m'-mu Adonai Eloheinu
וְהִשְׁתַּחֲווּ לְהַר קָדְשׁוֹ	and worship at His holy mountain,
	v'-hish-ta-cha-vu l'-har kad-sho
כִּי קָדוֹשׁ יהוה אֱלֹהֵינוּ:	for holy is Adonai our God.
	ki ka-dosh Adonai Eloheinu

*As the Torah Scroll is carried through the congregation,
everyone sings [in Hebrew]:*

כִּי מִצִּיּוֹן תֵּצֵא תוֹרָה	**For from Zion** will go forth the Torah
	ki mi-tzion tei-tzei torah
כִּי מִצִּיּוֹן תֵּצֵא תוֹרָה	For from Zion will go forth the Torah
	ki mi-tzion tei-tzei torah
וּדְבַר יהוה מִירוּשָׁלָיִם:[2]	and the word of Adonai from Jerusalem![2]
	u-d'-var Adonai mi-ru-sha-la-yim
בָּרוּךְ שֶׁנָּתַן תּוֹרָה	Blessed is He Who gave the Torah
	baruch she-na-tan torah
בָּרוּךְ שֶׁנָּתַן תּוֹרָה	Blessed is He Who gave the Torah
	baruch she-na-tan torah
לְעַמּוֹ יִשְׂרָאֵל	to His people, Israel
	l'-amo Yis-ra-el
בִּקְדֻשָּׁתוֹ:	in His holiness.
	bik-du-sha-to

*(Other songs may also be sung as the Torah Scroll is carried
throughout the Congregation on its way to the Bimah)*

אֵין כֵּאלֹהֵינוּ   There is None Like Our God

אֵין כֵּאלֹהֵינוּ	There is none like our God,
	ein kei-lo-hei-nu,
אֵין כַּאדוֹנֵינוּ	There is none like our Lord
	ein ka-do-nei-nu,
אֵין כְּמַלְכֵּנוּ	There is none like our King,
	ein k'-mal kei-nu,

(1) Ps 99:5 (2) Isaiah 2:3

Shabbat Morning Service

אֵין כְּמוֹשִׁיעֵנוּ There is none like our Savior.
ein k'-mo-shi-ei-nu.

מִי כֵאלֹהֵינוּ Who is like our God,
mi kei-lo hei-nu,

מִי כַאדוֹנֵינוּ Who is like our Lord,
mi ka-do-nei-nu,

מִי כְמַלְכֵּנוּ Who is like our King,
mi k'-mal-kei-nu,

מִי כְמוֹשִׁיעֵנוּ Who is like our Savior?
mi k'-mo-shi-ei-nu.

נוֹדֶה לֵאלֹהֵינוּ Let us give thanks to our God,
nodeh lei-lo-heinu,

נוֹדֶה לַאדוֹנֵינוּ Let us give thanks to our Lord,
nodeh la-do-nei-nu,

נוֹדֶה לְמַלְכֵּנוּ Let us give thanks to our King,
no-deh l'-mal-kei-nu

נוֹדֶה לְמוֹשִׁיעֵנוּ Let us give thanks to our Savior
no-deh l'-mo-shi-ei-nu.

בָּרוּךְ אֱלֹהֵינוּ Blessed be our God,
ba-ruch E-lo-hei-nu

בָּרוּךְ אֲדוֹנֵינוּ Blessed be our Lord,
ba-ruch A-do-nei-nu,

בָּרוּךְ מַלְכֵּנוּ Blessed be our King,
ba-ruch mal-ke-nu,

בָּרוּךְ מוֹשִׁיעֵנוּ Blessed be our Savior.
ba-ruch mo-shi-e-nu.

אַתָּה הוּא אֱלֹהֵינוּ Your are our God,
atah hu E-lo-hei-nu,

אַתָּה הוּא אֲדוֹנֵינוּ You are our Lord,
atah hu A-do-nei-nu,

אַתָּה הוּא מַלְכֵּינוּ You are our King,
atah hu mal-kei-nu,

אַתָּה הוּא מוֹשִׁיעֵנוּ You are our Savior
atah hu mo-shi-ei-nu.

אַתָּה הוּא You are the One
atah hu

שֶׁהִקְטִירוּ אֲבוֹתֵינוּ to whom our fathers
she-hik-ti-ru, a-vo-tei-nu,

לְפָנֶיךָ אֶת before You
l'-fa-ne-cha et

קְטֹרֶת הַסַּמִּים offered sweet smelling incense.
k'-to-ret ha-sa-mim.

Shabbat Morning Service

(Readers are called up to the Torah)

The Chazzan says:

מִי שֶׁבֵּרַךְ אֲבוֹתֵינוּ He who blessed our fathers
mi-she-bei-rach a-vo-teinu
אַבְרָהָם יִצְחָק וְיַעֲקֹב Abraham, Isaac, and Jacob,
Avraham, Yitz-chak, v'-Ya-a-kov
הוּא יְבָרֵךְ אֶת־ may He bless
hu y'-va-reich et

אֲשֶׁר עָלָה (עָלְתָה) who has come up
asher a-lah (al-tah)
לִכְבוֹד אֱלֹהִים וְהַתּוֹרָה to honor God and the Torah.
l'-kavod Elohim v'-ha-torah
הַקָּדוֹשׁ בָּרוּךְ הוּא May the Holy (blessed is He)
ha-ka-dosh baruch hu
יְבָרֵךְ אֹתוֹ (אֹתָהּ) bless him (her)
y'-va-reich oto (otah)
וְאֶת־מִשְׁפַּחְתּוֹ (מִשְׁפַּחְתָּהּ) and his (her) family
v'-et mish-pach-to (mish-pach-tah)
וְיִשְׁלַח בְּרָכָה וְהַצְלָחָה and send blessing and prosperity
v'-yish-lach b'-ra-cha v'-hatz-la-chah
בְּכָל־מַעֲשֵׂה יָדָיו (יָדֶיהָ) on all the work of his (her) hands.
b'-chol ma-a-seih ya-daiv (ya-de-ha)

Blessing before reading the Torah

בָּרְכוּ אֶת יהוה הַמְבֹרָךְ: Bless Adonai, Who is blessed
bar-chu et Adonai ha-m'-vo-rach

The congregation responds by saying:

בָּרוּךְ יהוה **Blessed** is Adonai
baruch Adonai
הַמְבֹרָךְ לְעוֹלָם וָעֶד: Who is blessed forever.
ha-m'-vo-rach l'-olam va-ed

Reader repeats this blessing then continues in Hebrew.
Congregation responds by reciting the blessing in English:

Shabbat Morning Service

בָּרוּךְ אַתָּה יהוה אֱלֹהֵינוּ
Blessed are You, Adonai our God
baruch ata Adonai Eloheinu

מֶלֶךְ הָעוֹלָם
King of the universe
melech ha-olam

אֲשֶׁר בָּחַר בָּנוּ
Who chose us
a-sher ba-char-banu

מִכָּל הָעַמִּים
from all the peoples
mi-kol ha-a-mim

וְנָתַן לָנוּ אֶת תּוֹרָתוֹ:
and gave to us His Torah.
v'-na-tan la-nu et to-ra-to

בָּרוּךְ אַתָּה יהוה
Blessed are You Adonai,
baruch ata Adonai

נוֹתֵן הַתּוֹרָה:
Giver of the Torah.
no-tein ha-torah

Blessing after reading the Torah. Reader recites in Hebrew and the Congregation responds by reciting the blessing in English:

בָּרוּךְ אַתָּה יהוה
Blessed are You Adonai
baruch ata Adonai

אֱלֹהֵינוּ מֶלֶךְ הָעוֹלָם
our God, King of the universe,
Eloheinu melech ha-olam

אֲשֶׁר נָתַן לָנוּ תּוֹרַת אֱמֶת
Who gave to us the Torah of truth
a-sher na-tan lanu to-rat e-met

וְחַיֵּי עוֹלָם נָטַע בְּתוֹכֵנוּ:
and planted everlasting life in our midst.
v'-cha-yei o-lam na-ta b'-to-cheinu

בָּרוּךְ אַתָּה יהוה
Blessed are you Adonai
baruch ata Adonai

נוֹתֵן הַתּוֹרָה:
Giver of the Torah.
no-tein ha-torah

Hagbah lifts the Torah for all to see, and the congregation proclaims (in Hebrew):

וְזֹאת הַתּוֹרָה אֲשֶׁר
This is the Torah which
v'-zot ha-torah asher

שָׂם מֹשֶׁה לִפְנֵי
Moses placed before the
sam Mo-she lif-nei

בְּנֵי יִשְׂרָאֵל[1]
children of Israel[1]
b'nei Yis-ra-el

עַל פִּי יהוה
upon the command of Adonai,
al pi Adonai

בְּיַד מֹשֶׁה:[2]
through the hand of Moses.[2]
b'-yad Mo-she

(1) Deut 4:44 (2) Num 9:23

Shabbat Morning Service

(Congregation continues to recite in English)

עֵץ חַיִּים הִיא	It is a tree of life
לַמַּחֲזִיקִים בָּהּ	*eitz cha-yim hi*
	to all who grasp it
	la-ma-cha-zi-kim bah
וְתֹמְכֶיהָ מְאֻשָּׁר:[1]	and its supporters are praiseworthy.[1]
	v'-to-m'-che-ha m'-u-shar
דְּרָכֶיהָ דַרְכֵי נֹעַם	Its ways are ways of pleasantness
	d'-ra-che-ha dar-chei no-am
וְכָל נְתִיבוֹתֶיהָ שָׁלוֹם[2]	and all its paths are peace.[2]
	v'-chol n'-ti-vo-te-ha shalom
אֹרֶךְ יָמִים בִּימִינָהּ	Long life is at its right,
	o-rech ya-mim bi-mi-nah
בִּשְׂמֹאלָהּ עֹשֶׁר וְכָבוֹד:[3]	at its left are riches and honor.[3]
	bis-mo-lah o-sher v'-cha-vod
יהוה חָפֵץ לְמַעַן	Adonai desired, for the sake of
	Adonai cha-feitz l'-ma-an
צִדְקוֹ	His righteousness,
	tzid-ko
יַגְדִּיל תּוֹרָה וְיַאְדִּיר:[4]	to make the Torah great and glorious.[4]
	yag-dil to-rah v'-ya-dir

Blessing before reading the Haftarah

בָּרוּךְ אַתָּה יהוה אֱלֹהֵינוּ	Blessed are You, Adonai our God,
	baruch ata Adonai Eloheinu
מֶלֶךְ הָעוֹלָם	King of the Universe,
	melech ha-olam
אֲשֶׁר בָּחַר בִּנְבִיאִים טוֹבִים	who chose good prophets,
	asher ba-char bin-vi-im to-vim
וְרָצָה בְדִבְרֵיהֶם	and was pleased with their words
	v'-ra-tzah b'-div-rei-hem
הַנֶּאֱמָרִים בֶּאֱמֶת	which they spoke in truth.
	ha-ne-e-ma-rim be-emet
בָּרוּךְ אַתָּה יהוה	Blessed are You Adonai,
	baruch ata Adonai
הַבּוֹחֵר בַּתּוֹרָה וּבְמֹשֶׁה	who chose the Torah, Moses
	ha-bo-cheir ba-to-rah u-v'-Mo-she
עַבְדּוֹ וּבְיִשְׂרָאֵל עַמּוֹ	His servant, Israel His people,
	av-do u-v'-Yis-ra-el a-mo
וּבִנְבִיאֵי הָאֱמֶת	and the prophets of truth
	u-vin-vi-ei ha-e-met
וָצֶדֶק	and righteousness.
	va-tze-dek

(1) Prov 3:18 (2) Prov 3:17 (3) Prov 3:16 (4) Is 42:21

Shabbat Morning Service

Blessing before reading the Apostolic Scriptures

בָּרוּךְ אַתָּה יהוה אֱלֹהֵינוּ Blessed are You, Adonai our God
baruch ata Adonai Eloheinu

מֶלֶךְ הָעוֹלָם King of the universe,
me-lech ha-o-lam

אֲשֶׁר נָתַן־לָנוּ אֶת דִּבְרֵי Who gave to us
a-sher na-tan la-nu

הַמָּשִׁיחַ יֵשׁוּעַ the words of Messiah Yeshua
et div-rei ha-ma-shi-ach Ye-shua

וְאֶת דִּבְרֵי שְׁלִיחָיו and the words of His apostles.
v'-et div-rei sh'-li-chaiv

בָּרוּךְ אַתָּה יהוה Blessed are You, Adonai,
baruch ata Adonai

נוֹתֵן אֶת דִּבְרֵי Giver of the words of
no-tein et div-rei

הַמָּשִׁיחַ יֵשׁוּעַ Messiah Yeshua.
ha-ma-shi-ach Ye-shua

Chazzan recites blessing after reading the Haftarah & Apostolic Scriptures

בָּרוּךְ אַתָּה יהוה אֱלֹהֵינוּ Blessed are You, Adonai our God,
baruch ata Adonai Eloheinu

מֶלֶךְ הָעוֹלָם King of the Universe,
me-lech ha-o-lam

צוּר כָּל הָעוֹלָמִים Rock of all the worlds,
tzur kol ha-o-la-mim

צַדִּיק בְּכָל הַדּוֹרוֹת Righteous in all the generations,
tza-dik b'-chol ha-dor-ot

הָאֵל הַנֶּאֱמָן the Almighty, the Faithful One,
ha-El ha-ne-e-man

הָאוֹמֵר וְעֹשֶׂה Who says and does,
ha-o-meir v'-o-seh

הַמְדַבֵּר וּמְקַיֵּם Who speaks and fulfills,
ham-da-beir u-m'-ka-yeim

שֶׁכָּל דְּבָרָיו אֱמֶת וָצֶדֶק: for all His words are true and right.
she-kol d'-va-raiv emet va-tzedek

נֶאֱמָן אַתָּה הוּא יהוה אֱלֹהֵינוּ Dependable are You, Adonai, our God,
ne-e-man ata hu Adonai Eloheinu

וְנֶאֱמָנִים דְּבָרֶיךָ and dependable are Your words,
v'-ne-e-ma-nim d'-va-reicha

וְדָבָר אֶחָד מִדְּבָרֶיךָ and not one of Your words
v'-da-var e-chad mi-d'-va-reicha

אָחוֹר לֹא יָשׁוּב רֵיקָם[1] is ever retracted unfulfilled,[1]
a-chor lo ya-shuv rei-kam

(1) cf. Is 55:11

Shabbat Morning Service

כִּי אֵל	for You are the Almighty,
	ki El
מֶלֶךְ נֶאֱמָן וְרַחֲמָן אָתָּה	a King who is dependable and merciful.
	me-lech ne-e-man v'-ra-cha-man ata
בָּרוּךְ אַתָּה יהוה הָאֵל	Blessed are You, Adonai, the Almighty
	baruch ata Adonai ha-El
הַנֶּאֱמָן בְּכָל דְּבָרָיו	who is dependable in all His words.
	ha-ne-e-man b'-chol d'va-raiv

Chazzan continues:

רַחֵם עַל צִיּוֹן	Have compassion on Zion
	ra-cheim al Tzi-yon
כִּי הִיא בֵּית חַיֵּינוּ	for it is the home of our life,
	ki hi beit cha-yei-nu
וְלַעֲלוּבַת נֶפֶשׁ	and the one whose soul is humiliated,
	v'-la-a-lu-vat ne-fesh
תּוֹשִׁיעַ בִּמְהֵרָה בְיָמֵינוּ	deliver speedily, in our days.
	to-shi-a bim-hei-rah v'-ya-meinu
בָּרוּךְ אַתָּה יהוה	Blessed are You, Adonai,
	baruch ata Adonai
מְשַׂמֵּחַ צִיּוֹן	Who causes Zion to rejoice
	m'-sa-mei-ach Tzi-yon
בְּבָנֶיהָ	with her children.
	b'-va-nei-ha
שַׂמְּחֵנוּ יהוה אֱלֹהֵינוּ	Cause us to rejoice, Adonai, our God,
	sa-m'-cheinu Adonai Eloheinu
בְּאֵלִיָּהוּ הַנָּבִיא עַבְדֶּךָ	with Elijah the prophet, Your servant,
	b'-Ei-li-ya-hu ha-na-vi av-decha
וּבְמַלְכוּת	and with the kingdom of the
	u-v'-mal-chut
בֵּית דָּוִד מְשִׁיחֶךָ	House of David, Your anointed.
	beit Da-vid m'-shi-che-cha
בִּמְהֵרָה יָבֹא	Speedily may He come
	bim-hei-rah ya-vo
וְיָגֵל לִבֵּנוּ	and cause our heart to exult.
	v'-ya-geil li-beinu
עַל כִּסְאוֹ לֹא יֵשֵׁב זָר	Upon his throne, no stranger will sit,
	al kis-o lo yei-sheiv zar
וְלֹא יִנְחֲלוּ עוֹד אֲחֵרִים	and others will no longer inherit
	v'-lo yin-cha-lo od a-chei-rim
אֶת כְּבוֹדוֹ	his honor.
	et k'-vo-do
כִּי בְשֵׁם קָדְשְׁךָ	For by Your holy Name,
	ki v'-sheim kad-sh'-cha

Shabbat Morning Service

נִשְׁבַּעְתָּ לוֹ You swore to Him
nish-ba-ta lo

שֶׁלֹּא יִכְבֶּה נֵרוֹ לְעוֹלָם וָעֶד that His light will never be extinguished.
she-lo yich-beh nei-ro l'-o-lam va-ed

בָּרוּךְ אַתָּה יהוה Blessed are You, Adonai,
baruch ata Adonai

מָגֵן דָּוִד shield of David.
ma-gein Da-vid

עַל הַתּוֹרָה וְעַל הָעֲבוֹדָה For the Torah, for the Divine Service,
al ha-to-rah v'-al ha-a-vo-dah

וְעַל הַנְּבִיאִים וְעַל הַשְּׁלָחִים for the prophets and apostles
v'-al ha-n'-vi-im v'-al ha-sh'-la-chim

וְעַל יוֹם הַשַּׁבָּת הַזֶּה and for this Sabbath Day
v'-al yom ha-sha-bat ha-ze

(When a Festival occurs on the Sabbath, add the appropriate line)

וְעַל יוֹם and for this day of
v'-al yom

חַג הַמַּצּוֹת הַזֶּה the Festival of Unleavened Bread
chag ha-ma-tzot ha-zeh

חַג הַשָּׁבוּעוֹת הַזֶּה the Festival of Shavuot
chag ha-sha-vu-ot ha-zeh

חַג יוֹם תְּרוּעַ הַזֶּה the Festival of Yom Teruah
chag yom te-ru-a ha-zeh

חַג הַסֻּכּוֹת הַזֶּה the Festival of Sukkot
chag ha-su-kot ha-zeh

הַשְּׁמִינִי חַג הָעֲצֶרֶת הַזֶּה the Festival of Shemini Atzeret
hash-mi-ni chag ha-a-tzeret ha-zeh

שֶׁנָּתַתָּ לָּנוּ יהוה אֱלֹהֵינוּ which You gave us, Adonai, our God,
she-na-ta-ta lanu Adonai Eloheinu

לִקְדֻשָּׁה וְלִמְנוּחָה for holiness and for rest,
lik-du-sha v'-lim-nu-chah

לְכָבוֹד וּלְתִפְאָרֶת for honor and for glory.
l'-cha-vod u-l'-tif-a-ret

עַל הַכֹּל יהוה אֱלֹהֵינוּ For all this, Adonai, our God,
al ha-kol Adonai Eloheinu

אֲנַחְנוּ מוֹדִים לָךְ we thank you,
a-nach-nu mo-dim lach

וּמְבָרְכִים אוֹתָךְ and bless You;
u-m'-var-chim o-tach

יִתְבָּרַךְ שִׁמְךָ בְּפִי blessed be Your Name by the mouth
yit-ba-rach shim-cha b'-fi

Shabbat Morning Service

כָּל חַי תָּמִיד לְעוֹלָם וָעֶד of all the living continually forever.
kol chai ta-mid l'-o-lam va-ed
בָּרוּךְ אַתָּה יהוה Blessed are You, Adonai,
baruch ata Adonai
מְקַדֵּשׁ הַשַּׁבָּת Sanctifier of the Sabbath.
m'-ka-deish ha-sha-bat

(On Festivals add)

וְיִשְׂרָאֵל וְהַזְּמַנִּים and Israel and the seasons
v'-Yis-ra-el v'-ha-z'-ma-nim

When the Torah is returned to the Ark, the following is said:

וּבְנֻחֹה יֹאמַר: **When the Ark rested** he would say,
u-v'-nu-choh yo-mar
שׁוּבָה יהוה Return, Adonai,
shu-vah Adonai
רִבְבוֹת אַלְפֵי יִשְׂרָאֵל to the myriad thousands of Israel.
riv-vot al-fei Yis-ra-el
קוּמָה יהוה Arise, Adonai,
ku-mah Adonai
לִמְנוּחָתֶךָ to Your resting place,
lim-nu-cha-techa
אַתָּה וַאֲרוֹן עֻזֶּךָ You and the Ark of Your might.
ata va-a-ron u-ze-cha
כֹּהֲנֶיךָ יִלְבְּשׁוּ Let Your priests be clothed
ko-ha-necha yil-b'-shu
צֶדֶק וַחֲסִידֶיךָ in righteousness and Your devout ones
tzedek va-cha-si-decha
יְרַנֵּנוּ.[1] will sing in joy.[1]
y'-ra-neinu
בַּעֲבוּר דָּוִד עַבְדֶּךָ For the sake of David Your servant
ba-a-vur Da-vid av-decha
אַל תָּשֵׁב פְּנֵי מְשִׁיחֶךָ do not reject the face of Your anointed.
al ta-sheiv p'-nei m'-shi-checha
כִּי לֶקַח טוֹב נָתַתִּי לָכֶם For I have given you good teaching
ki le-kach tov na-ta-ti la-chem
תּוֹרָתִי אַל תַּעֲזֹבוּ.[2] Do not forsake my Torah.[2]
to-ra-ti al ta-a-zo-vu

(1) Ps 132:8-10, cf. 2Chron 6:41 (2) Prov 4:2

Shabbat Morning Service

(Congregation sings this in Hebrew)

עֵץ חַיִּים הִיא	**It is a tree of life**
	eitz cha-yim hi
לַמַּחֲזִיקִים בָּהּ	to those who grasp it,
	la-ma-cha-zi-kim bah
וְתֹמְכֶיהָ מְאֻשָּׁר¹	and those who support it are blessed.¹
	v'-to-m'-che-ha m'-u-shar
דְּרָכֶיהָ דַרְכֵי נֹעַם	Its ways are pleasant ways
	d'-ra-che-ha dar-chei no-am
וְכָל נְתִיבוֹתֶיהָ שָׁלוֹם²	and all its paths are peace.²
	v'-chol n'-ti-vo-tei-ha shalom
הֲשִׁיבֵנוּ יהוה אֵלֶיךָ	Cause us to return to You, Adonai,
	ha-shi-veinu Adonai ei-leicha
וְנָשׁוּבָה	and we shall return.
	v'-na-shu-vah
חַדֵּשׁ יָמֵינוּ כְּקֶדֶם³	Renew our days as of old.³
	cha-deish ya-meinu k'-kedem

The Ark is closed

Chazzan says:

בָּרוּךְ אַתָּה יהוה	Blessed are You, Adonai
	ba-ruch ata Adonai
אֱלֹהֵינוּ מֶלֶךְ הָעוֹלָם	our God, King of the Universe,
	Eloheinu me-lech ha-o-lam
אֲשֶׁר נוֹתֵן לָנוּ	Who gives to us
	a-sher no-tein la-nu
אֶת הַדָּבָר הַחַיִּים	the Living Word
	et ha-d'-var ha-cha-yim
בְּיֵשׁוּעַ הַמָּשִׁיחַ	in Messiah Yeshua.
	b'-Ye-shu-a ha-Ma-shi-ach

(1) Prov 3:18 (2) Prov 3:17 (3) Lam 5:21

Shabbat Morning Service

אַשְׁרֵי Blessed

אַשְׁרֵי יוֹשְׁבֵי בֵיתֶךָ	Fortunate are those who dwell in Your house	Ash-rei yo-sheiv vei-techa
עוֹד יְהַלְלוּךָ סֶּלָה:[1]	May they always praise You. Selah[1]	od y'ha-l'-lucha selah
אַשְׁרֵי הָעָם שֶׁכָּכָה לוֹ	Fortunate the people whose lot is thus,	Ash-rei ha-am she-ka-cha lo
אַשְׁרֵי הָעָם שֶׁיהוה אֱלֹהָיו:[2]	Fortunate the people for whom Adonai is their God.[2]	Ash-rei ha-am she-Adonai Elohaiv
תְּהִלָּה לְדָוִד[3]	A Psalm of David[3]	t'hilah l'-David
אֲרוֹמִמְךָ אֱלוֹהַי הַמֶּלֶךְ	I will exalt You, my God, the King	a-ro-mim-cha Elohai ha-melech
וַאֲבָרְכָה שִׁמְךָ	and I will bless Your Name	va-a-va-r'-cha shim-cha
לְעוֹלָם וָעֶד:	forever and ever.	l'-olam va-ed
בְּכָל יוֹם אֲבָרְכֶךָּ	Every day I will bless You	b'-kol yom a-va-r'-checha
וַאֲהַלְלָה שִׁמְךָ	and extol Your Name	va-a-ha-l'-lah shim-cha
לְעוֹלָם וָעֶד:	forever and ever.	l'-olam va-ed
גָּדוֹל יהוה וּמְהֻלָּל מְאֹד	Adonai is great and highly extolled	Ga-dol Adonai u-m'-hu-lal m'-od
וְלִגְדֻלָּתוֹ אֵין חֵקֶר:	and His greatness is without measure.	v'-lig-du-la-to ein che-ker
דּוֹר לְדוֹר יְשַׁבַּח	Generation to generation will praise	Dor l'-dor y'-sha-bach
מַעֲשֶׂיךָ וּגְבוּרֹתֶיךָ	Your works and Your mighty acts	ma-a-sei-cha u-g'-vu-ro-techa
יַגִּידוּ:	they will declare.	ya-gidu
הֲדַר כְּבוֹד הוֹדֶךָ	Upon the splendor of Your glorious majesty	Ha-dar k'-vod ho-decha
וְדִבְרֵי נִפְלְאֹתֶיךָ	and the words of Your wonders	v'-div-rei nif-l'-otecha
אָשִׂיחָה:	I will meditate.	a-si-chah
וֶעֱזוּז נוֹרְאוֹתֶיךָ יֹאמֵרוּ	Of Your awesome acts they will speak.	v'-e-zuz no-ro-techa yo-mei-ru
וּגְדֻלָּתְךָ אֲסַפְּרֶנָּה:	And Your greatness I will recount.	u-g'-du-la-techa a-sa-p'-re-nah

(1) Ps 84:5 (2) Ps 144:15 (3) Ps 145

Shabbat Morning Service

זֵכֶר רַב טוּבְךָ	The memory of Your great goodness	
	zecher rav tu-v'-cha	
יַבִּיעוּ	they will eagerly tell,	
	ya-bi-u	
וְצִדְקָתְךָ	and of Your righteousness	
	v'-tzid-ka-t'-cha	
יְרַנֵּנוּ:	they will shout joyfully.	
	y'-ra-neinu.	
חַנּוּן וְרַחוּם יהוה	Adonai is gracious and compassionate,	
	cha-nun v'-ra-chum Adonai	
אֶרֶךְ אַפַּיִם וּגְדָל חָסֶד:	slow to anger and great in lovingkindness.	
	erech a-pa-yim u-g'-dol cha-sed.	
טוֹב יהוה לַכֹּל	Adonai is good to all	
	tov Adonai l'-kol	
וְרַחֲמָיו עַל כָּל	and His compassions are upon all of	
	v'-ra-cha-maiv al kol	
מַעֲשָׂיו:	His works.	
	ma-a-saiv.	
יוֹדוּךָ יהוה	They will give thanks to You, Adonai,	
	yo-ducha Adonai	
כָּל מַעֲשֶׂיךָ וַחֲסִידֶיךָ	all of Your works, and Your devoted ones	
	kol ma-a-secha va-cha-si-decha	
יְבָרְכוּכָה:	will bless You.	
	y'-var-chu-chah.	
כְּבוֹד מַלְכוּתְךָ	The glory of Your kingdom	
	k'-vod mal-chu-techa	
יֹאמֵרוּ וּגְבוּרָתְךָ	they will declare and of Your power	
	yo-mei-ru u-g'-vu-ra-t'-cha	
יְדַבֵּרוּ:	they will speak,	
	y'-da-bei-ru.	
לְהוֹדִיעַ לִבְנֵי הָאָדָם	to make known to the sons of men	
	l'-ho-dia liv-nei ha-a-dam	
גְּבוּרֹתָיו וּכְבוֹד הֲדַר	His power and the majestic glory	
	g'-vu-rotaiv u-ch'-vod ha-dar	
מַלְכוּתוֹ:	of His kingdom.	
	mal-chu-to.	
מַלְכוּתְךָ מַלְכוּת כָּל	Your kingdom is a kingdom for all	
	mal-chu-t'-cha mal-chut kol	
עוֹלָמִים וּמֶמְשַׁלְתְּךָ	time and Your rule is	
	o-la-mim u-mem-shal-t'-cha	
בְּכָל דֹּר וָדֹר:	in every generation.	
	b'-chol dor va-dor.	
סוֹמֵךְ יהוה לְכָל הַנֹּפְלִים	Adonai supports all who fall	
	so-meich Adoani l'-kol ha-no-f'-lim	

Shabbat Morning Service 92

וְזוֹקֵף לְכָל הַכְּפוּפִים:	and straightens all who are bent down.	v'-zo-keif l'-kol ha-k'-fu-fim.
עֵינֵי כֹל אֵלֶיךָ יְשַׂבֵּרוּ	The eyes of all look with hope to You	ei-nei chol ei-lecha y'-sa-beiru
וְאַתָּה נוֹתֵן לָהֶם	and You give to them	v'-ata no-tein la-hem
אֶת אָכְלָם בְּעִתּוֹ:	their food in due time.	et och-lam b'-ito.
פּוֹתֵחַ אֶת יָדֶךָ וּמַשְׂבִּיעַ	You open Your hand	po-tei-ach et ya-decha u-mas-bi-a
לְכָל חַי רָצוֹן:	and satisfy the desire of all the living.	l'-kol chai ra-tzon.
צַדִּיק יהוה בְּכָל דְּרָכָיו	Adonai is righteous in all His ways	tza-dik Adonai b'-chol d'-ra-chaiv
וְחָסִיד בְּכָל מַעֲשָׂיו:	and kind in everything He does.	v'-cha-sid b'-chol ma-a-saiv.
קָרוֹב יהוה לְכָל קֹרְאָיו	Adonai is near to all who call upon Him,	ka-rov Adonai l'-chol kor-aiv
לְכָל אֲשֶׁר יִקְרָאֻהוּ	to all who call upon Him	l'-chol asher yik-ra-u-hu
בֶאֱמֶת:	in truth.	ve-emet.
רְצוֹן יְרֵאָיו	The desire of those who fear Him	r'-tzon y'-rei-aiv
יַעֲשֶׂה וְאֶת שַׁוְעָתָם	He fulfills and their cry for help	ya-a-seh v'-et shav-a-tam
יִשְׁמַע וְיוֹשִׁיעֵם:	He hears and He delivers them.	yish-ma v'-yo-shi-eim.
שׁוֹמֵר יהוה אֶת כָּל אֹהֲבָיו	Adonai guards all who love Him	sho-mer Adonai et kol o-ha-vaiv
וְאֵת כָּל הָרְשָׁעִים	but all the wicked	v'-et kol ha-r'-sha-im
יַשְׁמִיד:	He will destroy.	yash-mid.
תְּהִלַּת יהוה יְדַבֶּר פִּי	Adonai's praise my mouth will speak	t'-hi-lat Adonai y'-daber pi
וִיבָרֵךְ כָּל בָּשָׂר	and all flesh will bless	vi-va-reich kol ba-sar
שֵׁם קָדְשׁוֹ לְעוֹלָם וָעֶד:	His holy Name forever and ever.	shem kad-sho l'-olam va-ed.
וַאֲנַחְנוּ נְבָרֵךְ יָהּ מֵעַתָּה	And we will bless God from now	va-a-nach-nu n'-ba-reich ya mei-ata
וְעַד עוֹלָם הַלְלוּיָהּ:[1]	and forever. Halleluyah!	v'-ad olam. Ha-l'-lu-yah.

(1) Ps 115:8

חֲצִי קַדִּישׁ Half Kaddish

(It is traditional to end a major section of the service by the Chazzan reciting the half kaddish)

יִתְגַּדַּל וְיִתְקַדַּשׁ	Exalted and sanctified
	yit-ga-dal v'-yit-ka-dash
שְׁמֵהּ רַבָּא בְּעָלְמָא דִּי	be His great Name in the world which
	sh'-mei raba b'-a-l'-ma di
בְרָא כִרְעוּתֵיהּ	He created according to His will,
	v'-ra chir-u-tei
וְיַמְלִיךְ מַלְכוּתֵיהּ	and may He rule His kingdom
	v'-yam-lich mal-chu-tei
בְּחַיֵּיכוֹן וּבְיוֹמֵיכוֹן	in your lifetime and in your days,
	b'-cha-yei-chon u-v'-yo-mei-chon
וּבְחַיֵּי דְכָל בֵּית	and in the lifetime of all the house
	u-v'-cha-yei d'-chol beit
יִשְׂרָאֵל בַּעֲגָלָא	of Israel, quickly,
	Yi-sra-el ba-a-ga-la
וּבִזְמַן קָרִיב וְאִמְרוּ אָמֵן:	and in the near future, and say, Amein.
	u-viz-man ka-riv v'-im-ru Amein.
יְהֵא שְׁמֵהּ רַבָּא מְבָרַךְ	May His great Name be blessed
	y'-hei sh'-mei ra-ba m'-va-rach
לְעָלַם וּלְעָלְמֵי עָלְמַיָּא:	forever and for ever.
	l'-a-lam u-l'-al-mei al-ma-ya
יִתְבָּרַךְ וְיִשְׁתַּבַּח וְיִתְפָּאַר	Blessed and praised, glorified
	yit-ba-rach v'-yish-ta-bach v'-yit-pa-ar
וְיִתְרוֹמַם וְיִתְנַשֵּׂא וְיִתְהַדָּר	and exalted and lifted up and honored
	v'-yit-ro-mam v'-yit-na-sei v'-yit-hadar
וְיִתְעַלֶּה וְיִתְהַלָּל	and elevated and extolled
	v'-yit-aleh v'-yit-halal
שְׁמֵהּ דְּקֻדְשָׁא	be the Name of the Holy One,
	sh'-mei d'-kud-sha
בְּרִיךְ הוּא	**He is blessed**,
	b'-rich hu
לְעֵלָּא (בעשית וּלְעֵלָּא מִכָּל)	above *(days of awe:* far above)
	l'-ei-la (u-l'-ei-la mi-chol)
מִן כָּל בִּרְכָתָא וְשִׁירָתָא	all the blessing and hymns,
	min kol bir-cha-ta v'-shir-a-ta
תֻּשְׁבְּחָתָא וְנֶחֱמָתָא	praises and consolations
	tush-b'-cha-ta v'-ne-che-ma-ta
דַּאֲמִירָן בְּעָלְמָא	which we say in the world
	da-a-mi-ran b'-a-l'-ma
וְאִמְרוּ אָמֵן:	and say, Amein
	v'-im-ru amein.

Shabbat Morning Service

עָלֵינוּ Aleinu (Alternative)

*(Congregation stands and sings in Hebrew, then recites in English
It is traditional to bow on the words "We therefore bow...")*

עָלֵינוּ לְשַׁבֵּחַ	**We are duty-bound** to praise
	a-lei-nu l'-sha-bei-ach
לַאֲדוֹן הַכֹּל	the Master of all
	la-adon ha-kol
לָתֵת גְּדֻלָּה	to ascribe greatness
	la-teit g'-du-lah
לְיוֹצֵר בְּרֵאשִׁית	to the One Who created from the beginning,
	l'-yo-tzeir b'-rei-shit
שֶׁהוּא קָרָא אוֹתָנוּ	that He called us
	she-hu ka-ra o-ta-nu
מִגּוֹיֵי הָאֲרָצוֹת	from the nations of the earth,
	mi-go-yei ha-a-ra-tzot
וּבָחַר בָּנוּ כְּמִשְׁפַּחְתּוֹ	and chose us as His family,
	u-va-char ba-nu k'-mish-pach-to
עַם סְגֻלָּה	a treasured people,
	am se-gu-lah
וְשָׂם חֶלְקֵנוּ בְּיֵשׁוּעַ	and placed our portion in Yeshua.
	v'-sam chel-kei-nu b'-Ye-shua
אֲנַחְנוּ עַמֶּךָ	We are Your people
	a-nach-nu a-me-cha
אֲשֶׁר פָּדִיתָ	whom You redeemed.
	a-sher pa-di-ta
וַאֲנַחְנוּ כּוֹרְעִים	We therefore bow
	va-a-nach-nu kor-im
וּמִשְׁתַּחֲוִים	and worship
	u-mish-ta-cha-vim
וּמוֹדִים לִפְנֵי מֶלֶךְ	and give thanks before the King,
	u-mo-dim lif-nei me-lech
מַלְכֵי הַמְּלָכִים	the King of Kings
	mal-chei ha-m'-la-chim
הַקָּדוֹשׁ בָּרוּךְ הוּא	the Holy One, blessed is He!
	ha-ka-dosh baruch hu
בַּיּוֹם הַהוּא	On that day
	ba-yom ha-hu
יִהְיֶה יהוה אֶחָד	Adonai will be One
	yih-yeh Adonai e-chad
וּשְׁמוֹ אֶחָד:[1]	and His Name One.[1]
	u-sh'-mo e-chad

(This Aleinu has been altered to emphasize our unity in Yeshua. For the traditional Aleinu, see next page.)

(1) Zech 14:9

עָלֵינוּ Aleinu (Traditional)

*(Congregation stands and sings in Hebrew, then recites in English
It is traditional to bow on the words "We therefore bow . . .")*

עָלֵינוּ לְשַׁבֵּחַ	We are duty-bound to praise
	a-lei-nu l'-sha-bei-ach
לַאֲדוֹן הַכֹּל	the Master of all
	la-adon ha-kol
לָתֵת גְּדֻלָּה	to ascribe greatness
	la-teit g'-du-lah
לְיוֹצֵר בְּרֵאשִׁית	to the One Who created from the beginning,
	l'-yo-tzeir b'-rei-shit
שֶׁלֹּא עָשָׂנוּ כְּגוֹיֵי	that He did not make us as the nations
	she-lo asanu k'-go-yei
הָאֲרָצוֹת וְלֹא שָׂמָנוּ	of the lands, and did not place us
	ha-a-ra-tzot v'-lo sa-manu
כְּמִשְׁפְּחוֹת הָאֲדָמָה	as the families of the earth;
	k'-mish-p'-chot ha-a-da-mah
שֶׁלֹּא שָׂם חֶלְקֵנוּ כָּהֶם	since He did not assign our portion as theirs
	she-lo sam chel-keinu ka-hem
וְגֹרָלֵנוּ כְּכָל הֲמוֹנָם.*	nor our lot like all of the masses.*
	v'-go-ra-leinu k'-chol ha-mo-nam
וַאֲנַחְנוּ כּוֹרְעִים	We therefore bow
	va-a-nach-nu kor-im
וּמִשְׁתַּחֲוִים	and worship
	u-mish-ta-cha-vim
וּמוֹדִים לִפְנֵי מֶלֶךְ	and give thanks before the King,
	u-mo-dim lif-nei me-lech
מַלְכֵי הַמְּלָכִים	the King of Kings
	mal-chei ha-m'-la-chim
הַקָּדוֹשׁ בָּרוּךְ הוּא.	the Holy One, blessed is He!
	ha-ka-dosh baruch hu
בַּיּוֹם הַהוּא	On that day
	ba-yom ha-hu
יִהְיֶה יהוה אֶחָד	Adonai will be One
	yih-yeh Adonai e-chad
וּשְׁמוֹ אֶחָד:	and His Name One.
	u-sh'-mo e-chad

(*) Original *Aleinu* included two additional lines here:[1]

שֶׁהֵם מִשְׁתַּחֲוִים לְהֶבֶל וָרִיק	For they bow to vanity and nothingness
	she-hem mish-ta-cha-vim l'-hevel va-rik
וּמִתְפַּלְלִים אֶל אֵל לֹא יוֹשִׁיעַ	and pray to a god who cannot save
	u-mit-pa-l'-lim el el lo yo-shi-a

(1) For the history, see *Art Scroll Siddur*, (nusach Ashkenaz), p. 159, notes.

Shabbat Morning Service

Let Us Adore

(Some Congregations sing "Let Us Adore" here.
Women echo the men.)

Men	Women
Let us adore	*Let us adore*
The everliving God	*The everliving God*
And render praise	*And render praise*
Unto Him	*Unto Him*
Who spread out the heavens	*Who spread out the heavens*
And established the earth	*And established the earth*
And Whose glory	*And Whose glory*
Is revealed in the heavens above	*Is revealed in the heavens above*
And Whose greatness	*And Whose greatness*

All Together
Is manifest throughout all the earth

Men	Women
He is our God	*He is our God*

All Together
There is none else!

קדיש יתום Mourner's Kaddish

(Chazzan and those observing yartzeit recite)

יִתְגַּדַּל וְיִתְקַדַּשׁ Exalted and sanctified
yit-ga-dal v'-yit-ka-dash
שְׁמֵהּ רַבָּא בְּעָלְמָא דִי be His great Name in the world which
sh'-mei ra-ba b'-al-ma di
בְּרָא כִרְעוּתֵיהּ He created according to His will
v'-ra chir-u-tei
וְיַמְלִיךְ מַלְכוּתֵיהּ and may He rule His kingdom
v'-yam-lich mal-chu-tei
בְּחַיֵּיכוֹן וּבְיוֹמֵיכוֹן in your lifetime and in your days,
b'-cha-yei-chon u-v'-yo-mei-chon
וּבְחַיֵּי דְכָל בֵּית and in the lifetime of all the house
u-v'-cha-yei d'-chol beit
יִשְׂרָאֵל בַּעֲגָלָא of Israel, quickly,
Yis-ra-el ba-a-ga-la
וּבִזְמַן קָרִיב and in the near future,
u-viz-man ka-riv
וְאִמְרוּ אָמֵן: and say, Amein.
v'-im-ru a-mein.

(All congregation recites)

יְהֵא שְׁמֵהּ רַבָּא מְבָרַךְ May His great Name be blessed
y'-hei sh'-mei ra-ba m'-va-rach
לְעָלַם וּלְעָלְמֵי עָלְמַיָּא: forever and for ever.
l'-a-lam u-l'-al-mei al-ma-ya

(Chazzan and those observing yartzeit continue)

יִתְבָּרַךְ וְיִשְׁתַּבַּח Blessed and praised
yit-ba-rach v'-yish-ta-bach
וְיִתְפָּאַר וְיִתְרוֹמַם glorified and exalted
v'-yit-pa-ar v'-yit-ro-mam
וְיִתְנַשֵּׂא וְיִתְהַדָּר and lifted up and honored
v'-yit-na-sei v'-yit-ha-dar
וְיִתְעַלֶּה וְיִתְהַלָּל and elevated and extolled
v'-yit-a-leh v'-yit-ha-lal

Shabbat Morning Service

שְׁמֵהּ דְּקֻדְשָׁא be the Name of the Holy One,
sh'-mei d'-kud-sha
בְּרִיךְ הוּא **He is blessed**,
b'-rich hu
לְעֵלָּא (בעשית) above (*days of awe:*
l'-ei-la
וּלְעֵלָּא מִכָּל) מִן כָּל far above) all the
(u-l'-ei-la mi-chol) min kol
בִּרְכָתָא וְשִׁירָתָא blessing and hymns,
bir-cha-ta v'-shi-ra-ta
תֻּשְׁבְּחָתָא וְנֶחֱמָתָא praises and consolations
tush-b'-cha-ta v'-ne-che-ma-ta
דַּאֲמִירָן בְּעָלְמָא which we say in the world
da-a-mi-ran b'-al-ma
וְאִמְרוּ אָמֵן: and say, Amein.
v'-im-ru a-mein.
יְהֵא שְׁלָמָא רַבָּא May there be much peace
y'-hei sh'-la-ma ra-ba
מִן שְׁמַיָּא וְחַיִּים טוֹבִים from heaven, and good life
min sh'-ma-ya v'-cha-yim to-vim
עָלֵינוּ וְעַל כָּל יִשְׂרָאֵל upon us and upon all Israel.
a-leinu v'-al kol Yis-ra-el
וְאִמְרוּ אָמֵן. and say, Amein.
v'-im-ru a-mein.
עֹשֶׂה שָׁלוֹם בִּמְרוֹמָיו[1] He Who makes peace in His heights[1]
O-sei sha-lom bim-ro-maiv
הוּא יַעֲשֶׂה שָׁלוֹם may He make peace
hu ya-a-sei sha-lom
עָלֵינוּ וְעַל כָּל יִשְׂרָאֵל upon us and upon all Israel.
a-lei-nu v'al kol Yis-ra-el
וְאִמְרוּ אָמֵן: and say, Amein.
v'-im-ru a-mein.

(*The Mourner's Kaddish contains no references to the dead. It is a prayer of praise and honor to God, recognizing that in His mysterious wisdom He does all things well. We commit ourselves to Him, even in times of deepest sorrow, knowing that He cares for us.*)

"Blessed be the God and Father of our Lord Yeshua Messiah,
the Father of mercies and God of all comfort,
who comforts us in all our affliction
so that we will be able to comfort those who are in any affliction
with the comfort with which we ourselves are comforted by God."[2]

(1) Job 25:2 (2) 2Cor 1:3–4

ברכת אהרן Aaronic Benediction

יְבָרֶכְךָ יהוה וְיִשְׁמְרֶךָ Adonai bless you and keep you.
y'-va-re-ch'-cha Adonai v'-yish-m'-recha

(קהל: כֵּן יְהִי רָצוֹן) (Cong: may it be His will)
ken y'-hi ra-tzon

יָאֵר יהוה פָּנָיו אֵלֶיךָ Adonai shine His face toward you
ya-eir Adonai pa-naiv ei-lecha

וִיחֻנֶּךָּ and be gracious to you.
vi-chu-necha

(קהל: כֵּן יְהִי רָצוֹן) (Cong: may it be His will)
ken y'-hi ra-tzon

יִשָּׂא יהוה פָּנָיו אֵלֶיךָ Adonai lift up His face toward you
yi-sa Adonai pa-naiv ei-lecha

וְיָשֵׂם לְךָ שָׁלוֹם and grant you peace.
v'-ya-seim l'cha shalom

(קהל: כֵּן יְהִי רָצוֹן)[1] (Cong: may it be His will)[1]
ken y'-hi ra-tzon

ברכת החודש Blessing for the New Month

יְהִי רָצוֹן מִלְּפָנֶיךָ May it be Your will,
y'-hi ra-tzon mi-l'-fa-necha

יהוה אֱלֹהֵינוּ וֵאלֹהֵי Adonai our God and God
Adonai Eloheinu vei-lo-hei

אֲבוֹתֵינוּ of our fathers,
a-vo-teinu

שֶׁתְּחַדֵּשׁ עָלֵינוּ that you renew for us
she-t'-cha-deish a-leinu

אֶת הַחֹדֶשׁ הַזֶּה this month
et ha-chodesh ha-zeh

לְטוֹבָה וְלִבְרָכָה for good and for blessing,
l'-tovah v'-liv-ra-chah

וְתִתֶּן לָנוּ חַיִּים אֲרוּכִים and grant us long life,
v'-ti-ten lanu cha-yim a-ru-chim

חַיִּים שֶׁל שָׁלוֹם a life of peace
cha-yim shel shalom

חַיִּים שֶׁל טוֹבָה a life of goodness
cha-yim shel tovah

חַיִּים שֶׁל בְּרָכָה a life of blessing
cha-yim shel b'-ra-chah

חַיִּים שֶׁל פַּרְנָסָה a life of sustenance
cha-yim shel par-na-sah

(1) Num 6:24–26

Shabbat Morning Service

חַיִּים שֶׁל חִלּוּץ עֲצָמוֹת	a life of physical strength
	cha-yim shel chi-lutz a-tza-mot
חַיִּים שֶׁיֵּשׁ בָּהֶם	a life in which there is
	cha-yim she-yeish ba-hem
יִרְאַת שָׁמַיִם וְיִרְאַת חֵטְא	fear of heaven and fear of sin
	yir-at sha-ma-im v'-yir-at cheit
חַיִּים שֶׁאֵין בָּהֶם	a life in which there is no
	cha-yim she-ein ba-hem
בּוּשָׁה וּכְלִמָּה	shame or disgrace,
	bu-shah uk-li-mah
חַיִּים שֶׁל עֹשֶׁר וְכָבוֹד	a life of prosperity and honor,
	cha-yim shel o-sher v'-cha-vod
חַיִּים שֶׁתְּהֵא בָנוּ	a life in which there will be
	cha-yim she-t'-hei vanu
אַהֲבַת תּוֹרָה	love of Torah
	a-ha-vat to-rah
וְיִרְאַת שָׁמַיִם	and fear of Heaven,
	v'-yir-at sha-ma-im
חַיִּים שֶׁיִּמָּלְאוּ	a life filled
	cha-yim she-yi-ma-l'-u
מִשְׁאֲלוֹת לִבֵּנוּ	with the wishes of our heart
	mish-a-lot li-beinu
לְטוֹבָה. אָמֵן סֶלָה:	for good. Amen Selah.
	l'-tovah amein selah
מִי שֶׁעָשָׂה נִסִּים	He who did miracles for our
	mi she-a-sah ni-sim
לַאֲבוֹתֵינוּ וְגָאַל אוֹתָם	fathers and redeemed them
	la-a-vo-teinu v'-ga-al o-tam
מֵעַבְדוּת לְחֵרוּת	from slavery to freedom.
	mei-av-dut l'-chei-rut
הוּא יִגְאַל אוֹתָנוּ בְּקָרוֹב	May He redeem us soon
	hu yig-al o-tanu b'-ka-rov
וִיקַבֵּץ נִדָּחֵינוּ	and gather our dispersed
	vi-ka-beitz ni-da-cheinu
מֵאַרְבַּע כַּנְפוֹת הָאָרֶץ	from the four corners of the earth;
	mei-ar-ba kan-fot ha-aretz
חֲבֵרִים כָּל יִשְׂרָאֵל	all Israel are companions!
	cha-vei-rim kol Yis-ra-el
וְנֹאמַר אָמֵן:	and let us say, Amen.
	v'-no-mar a-mein
רֹאשׁ חֹדֶשׁ _____	This new month of _____
	rosh chodesh
יִהְיֶה בְּיוֹם _____	which begins on _____
	yih-yeh b'-yom
הַבָּא עָלֵינוּ	may it come upon us
	ha-ba a-leinu

Havdalah

וְעַל כָּל יִשְׂרָאֵל לְטוֹבָה: and upon all Isarel for goodness.
v'-al kol Yis-ra-el l'-to-vah
יְחַדְּשֵׁהוּ הַקָּדוֹשׁ May He renew it, the Holy One,
y'-cha-d'-shei-hu ha-ka-dosh
בָּרוּךְ הוּא blessed is He,
ba-ruch hu
עָלֵינוּ וְעַל כָּל עַמּוֹ upon us and upon all His people
a-leinu v'-al kol a-mo
בֵּית יִשְׂרָאֵל the house of Israel
beit Yis-ra-el
לְחַיִּים וּלְשָׁלוֹם לְשָׂשׂוֹן for life, peace, happiness,
l'-cha-yim u-l'-shalom l'-sa-son
וּלְשִׂמְחָה and joy,
u-l'-sim-chah
לִישׁוּעָה וּלְנֶחָמָה for salvation and consolation,
li-shu-ah u-l'-ne-cha-mah
וְנֹאמַר אָמֵן: and let us say, Amen.
v'-no-mar a-mein

ברכות הבדלה Havdalah Blessings (Close of Sabbath)

הִנֵּה אֵל יְשׁוּעָתִי **Behold**, God is my salvation;
hi-nei El y'-shu-a-ti
אֶבְטַח וְלֹא אֶפְחָד I will trust and not be afraid
ev-tach v'-lo ef-chad
כִּי עָזִּי וְזִמְרָת For my strength and my song
ki a-zi v'-zim-rat
יָהּ יהוה is Yah Adonai
Ya Adonai
וַיְהִי לִי לִישׁוּעָה: and He is my salvation!
va-y'-hi li li-shu-ah
וּשְׁאַבְתֶּם מַיִם בְּשָׂשׂוֹן You can draw water with joy
u-sh'-av-tem ma-yim b'-sa-son
מִמַּעַיְנֵי הַיְשׁוּעָה:[1] from the wellsprings of salvation.[1]
mi-ma-ai-nei ha-y'-shu-ah
לַיהוה הַיְשׁוּעָה Salvation belongs to Adonai
la-donai ha-y'-shu-ah
עַל עַמְּךָ בִרְכָתֶךָ סֶּלָה:[2] upon Your people is your blessing. Selah[2]
al-a-m'-cha vir-cha-techa selah
יהוה צְבָאוֹת עִמָּנוּ Adonai of armies is with us
Adonai tz'-va-ot i-ma-nu
מִשְׂגָּב לָנוּ a stronghold for us
mis-gav lanu
אֱלֹהֵי יַעֲקֹב סֶלָה:[3] is the God of Jacob. Selah[3]
Elohei Ya-a-cov selah

(1) Is 12:2-3 (2) Ps 3:8 (3) Ps 46:8

Havdalah

יהוה צְבָאוֹת
Adonai of Armies—
Adonai tz'-va-ot

אַשְׁרֵי אָדָם בֹּטֵחַ בָּךְ:
blessed is the person who trusts in You!
ash-rei adam bo-tei-ach bach

יהוה הוֹשִׁיעָה
Adonai, save us!
Adonai ho-shi-ah

הַמֶּלֶךְ יַעֲנֵנוּ
The King will answer us
ha-melech ya-a-nei-nu

בְיוֹם קָרְאֵנוּ:
on the day we call.
v'-yom kar-einu

לַיְּהוּדִים הָיְתָה
For the Jews there was
la-y'-hu-dim ha-y'-tah

אוֹרָה וְשִׂמְחָה
light and gladness,
o-rah v'-sim-chah

וְשָׂשׂוֹן וִיקָר:
joy, and honor.
v'-sa-son vi-kar

כֵּן תִּהְיֶה לָנוּ
So may it be for us.
ken ti-h'-yeh lanu

כּוֹס יְשׁוּעוֹת אֶשָּׂא
The cup representing salvation I raise up
kos y'-shu-ot e-sah

וּבְשֵׁם יהוה אֶקְרָא:
and on the Name of Adonai I call out:
u-v'-shem Adonai ek-ra

Blessing for the wine

בָּרוּךְ אַתָּה יהוה
Blessed are You, Adonai
ba-ruch ata Adonai

אֱלֹהֵינוּ מֶלֶךְ הָעוֹלָם
our God, King of the Universe
Eloheinu me-lech ha-o-lam

בּוֹרֵא פְּרִי הַגָּפֶן
Creator of the fruit of the vine.
bo-rei p'-ri ha-ga-fen

Blessing for the spices

בָּרוּךְ אַתָּה יהוה
Blessed are You, Adonai
ba-ruch ata Adonai

אֱלֹהֵינוּ מֶלֶךְ הָעוֹלָם
our God, King of the Universe
Eloheinu me-lech ha-o-lam

בּוֹרֵא מִינֵי בְשָׂמִים:
Creator of all kinds of spices.
bo-rei mi-nei v'-sa-mim

Havdalah

Blessing for the light of the candle

בָּרוּךְ אַתָּה יהוה
Blessed are You, Adonai
ba-ruch ata Adonai
אֱלֹהֵינוּ מֶלֶךְ הָעוֹלָם
our God, King of the Universe,
Eloheinu me-lech ha-o-lam
בּוֹרֵא מְאוֹרֵי הָאֵשׁ:
Creator of the light of fire.
bo-rei m'-o-rei ha-eish

בָּרוּךְ אַתָּה יהוה
Blessed are You, Adonai
ba-ruch ata Adonai
אֱלֹהֵינוּ מֶלֶךְ הָעוֹלָם
our God, King of the Universe
Eloheinu me-lech ha-o-lam
הַמַּבְדִיל בֵּין קֹדֶשׁ
Who divides between holy and
ha-mav-dil bein ko-desh
לְחוֹל בֵּין אוֹר לְחֹשֶׁךְ
profane; between light and dark;
l'-chol bein or l'-cho-shech
בֵּין יִשְׂרָאֵל לָעַמִּים
between Israel and the peoples;
bein Yis-ra-el la-a-mim
בֵּין יוֹם הַשְּׁבִיעִי
between the seventh day
bein yom hash-vi-i
לְשֵׁשֶׁת יְמֵי הַמַּעֲשֶׂה:
and the six days of work.
l'-shei-shet y'-mei ha-ma-a-seh
בָּרוּךְ אַתָּה יהוה
Blessed are You, Adonai,
ba-ruch ata Adonai
הַמַּבְדִיל בֵּין
Who divides between
ha-mav-dil bein
קֹדֶשׁ לְחוֹל:
holy and profane.
ko-desh l'-chol

After extinguishing the candle in the wine,
Sing Shavuah Tov (hope for the new week) & Eliyahu HaNavi

שָׁבוּעַ טוֹב
A good week (repeats)
sha-vu-ah tov

A good week, a week of peace, may gladness reign,
and joy increase (repeat)

Eliyahu HaNavi

אֵלִיָּהוּ הַנָּבִיא
Elijah the prophet,
E-li-ya-hu ha-navi
אֵלִיָּהוּ הַתִּשְׁבִּי
Elijah the Tishbite
E-li-ya-hu haTishbi
אֵלִיָּהוּ אֵלִיָּהוּ
Elijah, Elijah,
E-li-ya-hu E-li-ya-hu

Havdalah

אֵלִיָּהוּ הַגִּלְעָדִי	Elijah the Gileadite *E-li-ya-hu ha-Gil-a-di*
בִּמְהֵרָה בְיָמֵינוּ	with haste, in our days *bim-hei-rah v'-ya-mei-nu*
יָבוֹא אֵלֵינוּ	may he come to us *ya-vo ei-lei-nu*
עִם מָשִׁיחַ בֶּן דָּוִד	with Messiah son of David *im Ma-shi-ach ben David*
עִם מָשִׁיחַ בֶּן דָּוִד	with Messiah son of David *im Ma-shi-ach ben David*
אֵלִיָּהוּ הַנָּבִיא	Elijah the prophet, *E-li-ya-hu ha-navi*
אֵלִיָּהוּ הַתִּשְׁבִּי	Elijah the Tishbite *E-li-ya-hu ha-Tish-bi*
אֵלִיָּהוּ אֵלִיָּהוּ	Elijah, Elijah, *E-li-ya-hu E-li-ya-hu*
אֵלִיָּהוּ הַגִּלְעָדִי	Elijah the Gileadite *E-li-ya-hu ha-Gil-a-di*

ברכת המפיל Prayer When Retiring at Night

בָּרוּךְ אַתָּה יהוה אֱלֹהֵינוּ
Blessed are You, Adonai our God
baruch ata Adonai Eloheinu

מֶלֶךְ הָעוֹלָם
King of the Universe
melech ha-olam

הַמַּפִּיל חֶבְלֵי שֵׁנָה
Who brings the fetters of sleep
ha-ma-pil chev-lei shei-nah

עַל עֵינַי וּתְנוּמָה
upon my eyes and slumber
al ei-nai u-t'-nu-mah

עַל עַפְעַפָּי
upon my eyelids.
al af-a-pai

וִיהִי רָצוֹן מִלְּפָנֶיךָ יהוה
May it be Your will, Adonai
vi-hi ra-tzon mi-l'-fa-neicha Adonai

אֱלֹהַי וֵאלֹהֵי אֲבוֹתַי
my God and God of my fathers,
Elohai vei-lo-hei a-vo-tai

שֶׁתַּשְׁכִּיבֵנִי לְשָׁלוֹם
that I lay down in peace
she-tash-ki-veini l'-shalom

וְתַעֲמִידֵנִי לְשָׁלוֹם
and rise up in peace.
v'-ta-a-mi-dei-ni l'-shalom

וְאַל יְבַהֲלוּנִי רַעְיוֹנַי
May no thoughts or evil terrify me,
v'-al y'-va-ha-lu-ni ra-yo-nai

וַחֲלוֹמוֹת רָעִים
nor bad dreams
va-cha-lo-mot ra-im

וְהִרְהוּרִים רָעִים
nor evil fancies (distrurb me).
v'-char-hu-rim ra-im

וּתְהֵא מִטָּתִי שְׁלֵמָה
And may my bed be perfect before You.[1]
u-t'-hei mi-ta-ti sh'-lei-mah l'-fa-neicha

לְפָנֶיךָ[1] וְהָאֵר עֵינַי
Enlighten my eyes again,
v'-ha-eir ei-nai

פֶּן אִישַׁן הַמָּוֶת
lest I sleep the sleep of death,
pen i-shan ha-ma-vet

כִּי אַתָּה הַמֵּאִיר
for You illumine
ki ata ha-mei-ir

לְאִישׁוֹן בַּת עָיִן
the pupil of the eye.
l'-i-shon bat a-yin

בָּרוּךְ אַתָּה יהוה
Blessed are You, Adonai,
baruch ata Adonai

הַמֵּאִיר לָעוֹלָם כֻּלּוֹ
Who illumines the whole world
ha-mei-ir la-olam ku-lo

בִּכְבוֹדוֹ
with His glory.
bich-vo-do

---

(1) See Rashi on Genesis 47:31 where he interprets the "head of the bed" upon which Jacob leaned as referring to the Divine Presence.

Prayer When Retiring at Night

אֵל מֶלֶךְ נֶאֱמָן
Almighty, faithful King—
El melech ne-e-man

שְׁמַע יִשְׂרָאֵל
Hear, O Israel,
Shema Yis-ra-el

יהוה אֱלֹהֵינוּ יהוה אֶחָד:
Adonai is our God, Adonai is one!
Adonai Eloheinu Adonai echad

בָּרוּךְ שֵׁם כְּבוֹד
Blessed is the Name! The glory of
baruch shem k'-vod

מַלְכוּתוֹ לְעוֹלָם וָעֶד
His kingdom is for all eternity.
mal-chu-to l'-olam va-ed

וְאָהַבְתָּ אֵת יהוה אֱלֹהֶיךָ
And you shall love Adonai Your God
v'-a-hav-ta et Adonai Elohei-cha

בְּכָל־לְבָבְךָ וּבְכָל־נַפְשְׁךָ
with all your heart and with all your soul
b'-chol l'-vav-cha u-v'-chol naf-sh'-cha

וּבְכָל־מְאֹדֶךָ
and with all your might.
u-v'-chol m'-o-decha

וְהָיוּ הַדְּבָרִים הָאֵלֶּה אֲשֶׁר
These words which
v'-ha-yu ha-d'-va-rim ha-ei-le asher

אָנֹכִי מְצַוְּךָ הַיּוֹם
I command you today shall be
a-nochi m'-tza-v'-cha ha-yom

עַל־לְבָבֶךָ:
on your heart.
al l'-va-vecha

וְשִׁנַּנְתָּם
And you shall teach them diligently
v'-shi-nan-tam

לְבָנֶיךָ וְדִבַּרְתָּ בָּם
to your children and speak of them
l'-va-necha v'-di-bar-ta bam

בְּשִׁבְתְּךָ בְּבֵיתֶךָ
when you sit in your house,
b'-shiv-t'-cha b'-vei-techa

וּבְלֶכְתְּךָ בַדֶּרֶךְ
when you travel on the road
u-v'-lech-t'-cha va-derech

וּבְשָׁכְבְּךָ וּבְקוּמֶךָ
and when you lie down and rise up.
u-v'-shach-b'-cha u-v'-ku-mecha

וּקְשַׁרְתָּם לְאוֹת
Bind them for a sign
u-k'-shar-tam l'-ot

עַל־יָדֶךָ וְהָיוּ
upon your hand and they shall be
al ya-decha v'-ha-yu

לְטֹטָפֹת בֵּין עֵינֶיךָ
for *tefillin* between your eyes
l'-to-ta-fot bein ei-neicha

וּכְתַבְתָּם עַל מְזֻזוֹת
and write them upon the doorposts
u-ch'-tav-tam al m'-zu-zot

בֵּיתֶךָ וּבִשְׁעָרֶיךָ:[1]
of your house and upon your gates.[1]
bei-techa u-vish-a-reicha

(1) Deut 6:4ff

Prayer When Retiring at Night

וִיהִי נֹעַם אֲדֹנָי	May the friendship of Adonai	vi-hi no-am Adonai
אֱלֹהֵינוּ עָלֵינוּ	our God be upon us,	Eloheinu a-leinu
וּמַעֲשֵׂה יָדֵינוּ	and the work of our hands	u-ma-a-seih ya-dei-nu
כּוֹנְנָה עָלֵינוּ	establish for us,	ko-n'-na a-leinu
וּמַעֲשֵׂה יָדֵינוּ כּוֹנְנֵהוּ[1]	and the work of our hands establish![1]	u-ma-a-seih ya-deinu ko-n'-nei-hu
יֹשֵׁב בְּסֵתֶר[2]	He who dwells in the shelter[2]	yo-sheiv b'-sei-ter
עֶלְיוֹן בְּצֵל	of the Almighty, in the shadow of	El-yon b'-tzeil
שַׁדַּי יִתְלוֹנָן	Shaddai he will abide.	Sha-dai yit-lo-nan
אֹמַר לַיהוה	I say of Adonai,	o-mar la-donai
מַחְסִי וּמְצוּדָתִי	He is my refuge and my fortress,	mach-si u-m'-tzu-da-ti
אֱלֹהַי אֶבְטַח בּוֹ	my God in whom I trust.	Elohai ev-tach bo
כִּי הוּא יַצִּילְךָ מִפַּח יָקוּשׁ	For He will deliver you from the snare,	ki hu ya-tzi-l'-cha mi-pach ya-kush
מִדֶּבֶר הַוּוֹת	from the destructive pestilence.	mi-dever ha-vot
בְּאֶבְרָתוֹ יָסֶךְ לָךְ	With His wings He will cover you	b'-ev-ra-to ya-sech lach
וְתַחַת כְּנָפָיו תֶּחְסֶה	and under His wings you will be secure.	v'-ta-chat k'-na-faiv tech-seh
צִנָּה וְסֹחֵרָה אֲמִתּוֹ	A shield, a full shield is His truth.	tzi-nah v'-so-chei-rah a-mito
לֹא תִירָא מִפַּחַד לָיְלָה	You will not fear the terror at night	lo ti-ra mi-pa-chad la-y'-lah
מֵחֵץ יָעוּף יוֹמָם	nor the arrow that flies by day,	mei-cheitz ya-uf yo-mam
מִדֶּבֶר בָּאֹפֶל יַהֲלֹךְ	the pestilence that prowls in the dark,	mi-dever ba-o-fel ya-ha-loch
מִקֶּטֶב	nor the deadly pestilence	mi-ketev
יָשׁוּד צָהֳרָיִם	that destroys at noon.	ya-shud tza-ho-ra-im
יִפֹּל מִצִּדְּךָ אֶלֶף	A thousand will fall at your left side,	yi-pol mi-tzi-d'-cha elef

(1) Ps 90:17 (2) Ps 91

Prayer When Retiring at Night

וּרְבָבָה מִימִינֶךָ
ten thousand at your right side,
u-r'-va-vah mi-mi-necha

אֵלֶיךָ לֹא יִגָּשׁ
but it will not come near you.
ei-leicha lo yi-gash

רַק בְּעֵינֶיךָ תַבִּיט
Only with your eyes you will see it
rak b'-ei-neicha ta-bit

וְשִׁלֻּמַת רְשָׁעִים תִּרְאֶה
and view the punishment of the wicked.
v'-shi-lu-mat r'-sha-im tir-eh

כִּי אַתָּה יהוה מַחְסִי
For You, Adonai, are my refuge;
ki ata Adonai mach-si

עֶלְיוֹן שַׂמְתָּ מְעוֹנֶךָ
You have made the Most High your dwelling.
Elyon sam-ta m'-o-necha

לֹא תְאֻנֶּה אֵלֶיךָ רָעָה
No evil will befall you,
lo t'-u-neh ei-leicha ra-ah

וְנֶגַע לֹא יִקְרַב בְּאָהֳלֶךָ
nor a plague come near your tent.
v'-ne-ga lo yik-rav b'-a-ho-lecha

כִּי מַלְאָכָיו יְצַוֶּה לָּךְ
For He will command His angels for you
ki-mal-a-chaiv y'-tza-veh lach

לִשְׁמָרְךָ בְּכָל דְּרָכֶיךָ
to keep you in all your ways.
lish-ma-r'-cha b'-chol d'-ra-che-cha

עַל כַּפַּיִם יִשָּׂאוּנְךָ
They will carry you on their hands
al ka-pa-im yi-sa-u-n'-cha

פֶּן תִּגֹּף בָּאֶבֶן רַגְלֶךָ
lest you strike your foot on a stone.
pen ti-gof ba-even rag-lecha

עַל שַׁחַל וָפֶתֶן תִּדְרֹךְ
Upon lion and snake you will tread,
al sha-chal va-feten tid-roch

תִּרְמֹס כְּפִיר וְתַנִּין
you will trample young lion and serpent.
tir-mos k'-fir v'-ta-nin

כִּי בִי חָשַׁק וַאֲפַלְּטֵהוּ
For to Me he clings, so I will save him.
ki vi cha-shak va-a-fa-l'-teihu

אֲשַׂגְּבֵהוּ כִּי יָדַע שְׁמִי
I will strengthen him for he knows My Name.
a-sa-g'-veihu ki ya-da sh'-mi

יִקְרָאֵנִי וְאֶעֱנֵהוּ
He will call to Me and I will answer him;
yik-ra-ei-ni v'-e-e-neihu

עִמּוֹ אָנֹכִי בְצָרָה
I am with him in distress.
i-mo a-no-chi v'-tza-rah

אֲחַלְּצֵהוּ וַאֲכַבְּדֵהוּ
I will free him and honor him.
a-cha-l'-tzeihu va-a-cha-b'-deihu

אֹרֶךְ יָמִים אַשְׂבִּיעֵהוּ
With length of days I will satisfy him,
orech ya-mim as-bi-ei-hu

וְאַרְאֵהוּ בִּישׁוּעָתִי
and show him My salvation;
v'-ar-eihu bi-shu-a-ti

אֹרֶךְ יָמִים אַשְׂבִּיעֵהוּ
With length of days I will satisfy him,
orech ya-mim as-bi-ei-hu

Prayer When Retiring at Night

Psalm 3

וְאַרְאֵהוּ בִּישׁוּעָתִי	and show him My salvation.
	v'-ar-eihu bi-shu-a-ti
יהוה מָה רַבּוּ צָרָי	Adonai, how many are my tormentors!
	Adonai mah ra-bu tza-rai
רַבִּים קָמִים עָלָי רַבִּים	Many are rising up against me.
	ra-bim ka-mim a-lai ra-bim
אֹמְרִים לְנַפְשִׁי	They are saying about me,
	om-rim l'-naf-shi
אֵין יְשׁוּעָתָה לּוֹ בֵאלֹהִים	There is no deliverance for him in God.
	ein y'-shu-a-ta lo vei-lo-him
סֶלָה	Selah.
	selah
וְאַתָּה יהוה מָגֵן בַּעֲדִי	But You, Adonai, are a shield about me,
	v'-ata Adonai ma-gein ba-a-di
כְּבוֹדִי וּמֵרִים רֹאשִׁי	My glory, and the One who lifts my head.
	k'-vo-di u-mei-rim ro-shi
קוֹלִי אֶל יהוה אֶקְרָא	I cried out to Adonai with my voice,
	ko-li el Adonai ek-ra
וַיַּעֲנֵנִי	And He answered me
	va-ya-a-nei-ni
מֵהַר קָדְשׁוֹ סֶלָה	from His holy mountain. Selah.
	mei-har kad-sho selah
אֲנִי שָׁכַבְתִּי וָאִישָׁנָה	I lay down and slept;
	ani sha-chav-ti va-i-sha-nah
הֱקִיצוֹתִי	I awoke,
	he-ki-tzo-ti
כִּי יהוה יִסְמְכֵנִי	for Adonai sustains me.
	ki Adonai yis-m'-chei-ni
לֹא אִירָא מֵרִבְבוֹת עָם	I will not fear ten thousands of people
	lo i-ra mei-riv-vot am
אֲשֶׁר סָבִיב שָׁתוּ עָלָי	deployed against me on every side.
	asher sa-viv sha-tu a-lai
קוּמָה יהוה הוֹשִׁיעֵנִי	Arise, Adonai; save me,
	ku-mah Adonai ho-shi-eini
אֱלֹהַי כִּי הִכִּיתָ	O my God! For You have smitten
	Elohai ki hi-ki-ta
אֶת כָּל אֹיְבַי לֶחִי	all my enemies on the cheek;
	et kol o-y'-vai le-chi
שִׁנֵּי רְשָׁעִים	the teeth of the wicked
	shi-nei r'-sha-im
שִׁבַּרְתָּ	You have shattered.
	shi-bar-ta

Prayer When Retiring at Night

לַיהוה הַיְשׁוּעָה
Salvation belongs to Adonai;
la-donai ha-y'-shu-ah

עַל עַמְּךָ בִרְכָתֶךָ סֶּלָה
upon Your people is Your blessing, selah.
al a-m'-cha vir-cha-techa selah

הַשְׁכִּיבֵנוּ יהוה אֱלֹהֵינוּ
Cause us to lie down, Adonai our God,
hash-ki-veinu Adonai Eloheinu

לְשָׁלוֹם וְהַעֲמִידֵנוּ מַלְכֵּנוּ
in peace, and raise us again, our King,
l'-shalom v'-ha-a-mi-deinu mal-cheinu

לְחַיִּים
to life.
l'-cha-yim

וּפְרוֹשׂ עָלֵינוּ סֻכַּת
Spread over us the shelter
u-f'-ros a-leinu su-kat

שְׁלוֹמֶךָ
of Your shalom
sh'-lo-mecha

וְתַקְּנֵנוּ בְּעֵצָה טוֹבָה
and establish us in the good counsel
v'-ta-k'-neinu b'-ei-tza to-vah

מִלְּפָנֶיךָ
from Your presence.
mi-l'-fa-neicha

וְהוֹשִׁיעֵנוּ לְמַעַן שְׁמֶךָ
Save us for Your Name's sake
v'-ho-shi-einu l'-ma-an sh'-mecha

וְהָגֵן בַּעֲדֵנוּ
and shield us.
v'-ha-gein ba-a-deinu

וְהָסֵר מֵעָלֵינוּ אוֹיֵב דֶּבֶר
Remove from us enemy, pestilence,
v'-ha-seir mei-a-leinu o-yeiv dever

חֶרֶב וְרָעָב וְיָגוֹן
sword, famine, and sorrow.
v'-cherev v'-ra-av v'-ya-gon

וְהָסֵר שָׂטָן מִלְּפָנֵינוּ
Remove the adversary from before us,
v'-ha-seir sa-tan mi-l'-fa-neicha

וּמֵאַחֲרֵינוּ
and from behind us,
u-mei-a-cha-reinu

וּבְצֵל כְּנָפֶיךָ
and in the shadow of Your wings
u-v'-tzeil k'-na-feicha

תַּסְתִּירֵנוּ כִּי אֵל
protect us, for You are the Almighty
tas-ti-reinu ki El

שׁוֹמְרֵנוּ וּמַצִּילֵנוּ אָתָּה
Who guards and delivers us.
sho-m'-reinu u-ma-tzi-leinu ata

כִּי אֵל מֶלֶךְ
Surely You are the Almighty, King,
ki El melech

חַנּוּן וְרַחוּם אָתָּה
gracious and merciful.
cha-nun v'-ra-chum ata

וּשְׁמֹר צֵאתֵנוּ וּבוֹאֵנוּ
Guard our going out and coming in
u-sh'-mor tzei-teinu u-vo-einu

לְחַיִּים וּלְשָׁלוֹם מֵעַתָּה
for life and peace, from now
l'-cha-yim u-l'-shalom mei-a-tah

and forever.[1]

(1) Ps 121:8

Prayer When Retiring at Night

בָּרוּךְ יהוה בַּיּוֹם	Blessed is Adonai in the day; *baruch Adonai ba-yom*
בָּרוּךְ יהוה בַּלַּיְלָה	Blessed is Adonai in the night; *baruch Adonai ba-la-y'-lah*
בָּרוּךְ יהוה בְּשָׁכְבֵנוּ	Blessed is Adonai when we lie down; *baruch Adonai b'-shach-veinu*
בָּרוּךְ יהוה בְּקוּמֵנוּ	Blessed is Adonai when we rise up. *baruch Adonai b'-ku-meinu*
כִּי בְיָדְךָ נַפְשׁוֹת	For in Your hand are the souls *ki v'-ya-d'-cha naf-shot*
הַחַיִּים וְהַמֵּתִים	of the living and the dead: *ha-cha-yim v'-ha-mei-tim*
אֲשֶׁר בְּיָדוֹ נֶפֶשׁ כָּל חָי	In His hand is the soul of every life *asher b'-ya-do nefesh kol chai*
וְרוּחַ כָּל בְּשַׂר אִישׁ[1]	and the spirit of every human being.[1] *v'-ru-ach kol b'-sar ish*
בְּיָדְךָ אַפְקִיד רוּחִי[2]	Into Your hand I commit my spirit;[2] *b'-ya-d'-cha af-kid ru-chi*
פָּדִיתָה אוֹתִי	You have liberated me, *pa-di-tah o-ti*
יהוה אֵל אֱמֶת	Adonai, God of truth. *Adonai El emet*
אֱלֹהֵינוּ שֶׁבַּשָּׁמַיִם	Our God Who is in heaven, *Eloheinu she-ba-sha-ma-im*
יַחֵד שִׁמְךָ	make Your Name one *ya-cheid shim-cha*
וְקַיֵּם מַלְכוּתְךָ תָּמִיד	and establish Your kingdom always, *v'-ka-yeim mal-chu-t'-cha ta-mid*
וּמְלוֹךְ עָלֵינוּ לְעוֹלָם וָעֶד	and rule over us forever and ever. *u-m'-loch a-leinu l'-olam va-ed*
יִרְאוּ עֵינֵינוּ וְיִשְׂמַח	May our eyes see and our heart rejoice, *yir-u ei-neinu v'-is-mach li-beinu*
לִבֵּנוּ וְתָגֵל נַפְשֵׁנוּ	and our souls exalt *v'-ta-geil naf-sheinu*
בִּישׁוּעָתְךָ בֶּאֱמֶת	in Your salvation in truth, *bi-shu-a-t'-cha be-emet*
בֶּאֱמֹר לְצִיּוֹן	when it will be said in Zion, *be-e-mor l'-Tzi-yon*
מָלַךְ אֱלֹהָיִךְ[3]	"Your God reigns!"[3] *ma-lach E-lo-ha-yich*
יהוה מֶלֶךְ יהוה מָלָךְ[4]	Adonai is King, Adonai was King,[4] *Adonai melech Adonai malach*
	Adonai will be King forever and ever.[5] *Adonai yim-loch l'-olam va-ed*

וְעֶד עוֹלָם[1]

(1) Job 12:10 (2) Ps 31:5 (3) Is 52:7 (4) cf. Ps 10:16; 93:1 (5) Ex 15:18

Prayer When Retiring at Night

יהוה יִמְלֹךְ לְעֹלָם וָעֶד׃[5]
For the Kingdom is Yours
ki ha-mal-chut she-l'-cha hi
כִּי הַמַּלְכוּת שֶׁלְּךָ הִיא
and to all eternity You will reign
u-l'-o-l'-mei ad tim-loch
וּלְעוֹלְמֵי עַד תִּמְלוֹךְ
in glory, for we have no King
b'-cha-vod ki ein lanu melech
בְּכָבוֹד כִּי אֵין לָנוּ מֶלֶךְ
but You.
e-la ata
אֶלָּא אָתָּה
The Angel who redeemed me
ha-mal-ach ha-go-eil o-ti
הַמַּלְאָךְ הַגֹּאֵל אֹתִי
from all evil, may He bless
mi-kol ra y'-va-reich et
מִכָּל רָע יְבָרֵךְ אֶת
the lads and may they be called
ha-n'-a-rim v'-yi-ka-rei va-hem
הַנְּעָרִים וְיִקָּרֵא בָהֶם
by my name and the name of my fathers,
sh'-mi v'-sheim a-vo-tai
שְׁמִי וְשֵׁם אֲבוֹתַי
Abraham and Isaac,
Avraham v'-Yitz-chak
אַבְרָהָם וְיִצְחָק
and may they multiply like fish
v'-yid-gu la-rov
וְיִדְגּוּ לָרֹב
in the midst of the Land.[1]
b'-kerev ha-aretz
בְּקֶרֶב הָאָרֶץ׃[1]
And He said, "If you will diligently heed
va-yo-mer im sha-mo-a tish-ma
וַיֹּאמֶר אִם שָׁמוֹעַ תִּשְׁמַע
the voice of Adonai your God,
l'-kol Adonai Eloheicha
לְקוֹל יהוה אֱלֹהֶיךָ
and do what is upright in His eyes,
v'-ha-ya-shar b'-ei-naiv ta-a-seh
וְהַיָּשָׁר בְּעֵינָיו תַּעֲשֶׂה
and listen to His commandments,
v'-ha-a-zan-ta l'-mitz-vo-taiv
וְהַאֲזַנְתָּ לְמִצְוֹתָיו
and guard all His statutes,
v'-sha-mar-ta kol chu-kaiv
וְשָׁמַרְתָּ כָּל חֻקָּיו
then all the sickness which I put
kol ha-ma-cha-lah asher sam-ti
כָּל הַמַּחֲלָה אֲשֶׁר שַׂמְתִּי
in Egypt I will not put upon you,
v'-mitz-ra-yim lo a-sim a-leicha
בְמִצְרַיִם לֹא אָשִׂים עָלֶיךָ
for I am Adonai your Healer."[2]
ki ani Adonai ro-f'-echa
כִּי אֲנִי יהוה רֹפְאֶךָ׃[2]
And Adonai said to Satan,
va-yomer Adonai el ha-sa-tan
וַיֹּאמֶר יהוה אֶל הַשָּׂטָן
"Adonai rebukes you, Satan!
yig-ar Adonai b'-cha ha-sa-tan
יִגְעַר יהוה בְּךָ הַשָּׂטָן
Adonai rebukes you—
v'-yig-ar Adonai b'-cha
וְיִגְעַר יהוה בְּךָ
The One Who chose Jerusalem.
ha-bo-cheir bi-ru-sha-la-im

(1) Gen 48:16 (2) Ex 15:26

113 — Prayer When Retiring at Night

הַבֹּחֵר בִּירוּשָׁלָיִם
הֲלוֹא זֶה אוּד
מֻצָּל מֵאֵשׁ:¹

For is this one not a firebrand
ha-lo zeh ud
plucked from the fire?"[1]
mu-tzal mei-eish

יְבָרֶכְךָ יהוה וְיִשְׁמְרֶךָ:
יָאֵר יהוה פָּנָיו אֵלֶיךָ
וִיחֻנֶּךָ:
יִשָּׂא יהוה פָּנָיו אֵלֶיךָ
וְיָשֵׂם לְךָ שָׁלוֹם:²

Adonai bless you and keep you.
y'-va-re-ch'-cha Adonai v'-yish-m'-recha
Adonai shine His face toward you
ya-eir Adonai pa-naiv ei-lecha
and be gracious to you.
vi-chu-necha
Adonai lift up His face toward you
yi-sa Adonai pa-naiv ei-lecha
and grant you peace.[2]
v'-ya-seim l'-cha shalom

הִנֵּה לֹא יָנוּם וְלֹא יִישָׁן
שׁוֹמֵר יִשְׂרָאֵל:³

Behold, He neither slumbers nor sleeps,
hi-nei lo ya-num v'-lo yi-shan
The Keeper of Israel![3]
sho-mer Yis-rael

לִישׁוּעָתְךָ קִוִּיתִי יהוה⁴
קִוִּיתִי לִישׁוּעָתְךָ יהוה
יהוה לִישׁוּעָתְךָ קִוִּיתִי:

For Your salvation I hope, Adonai;[4]
li-shu-a-t'-cha ki-vi-ti Adonai
I hope for Your salvation, Adonai;
ki-vi-ti li-shu-a-t'-cha Adonai
Adonai, for Your salvation I hope!
Adonai li-shu-a-t'-cha ki-vi-ti

Psalm 128

שִׁיר הַמַּעֲלוֹת
אַשְׁרֵי כָּל יְרֵא יהוה
הַהֹלֵךְ בִּדְרָכָיו
יְגִיעַ כַּפֶּיךָ כִּי תֹאכֵל
אַשְׁרֶיךָ
וְטוֹב לָךְ:
אֶשְׁתְּךָ כְּגֶפֶן פֹּרִיָּה

A Song of Ascents.
shir ha-ma-a-lot
How blessed are all who fear Adonai,
ash-rei kol y'-rei Adonai
Who walk in His ways.
ha-ho-leich bid-ra-chaiv
When you eat of the fruit of your hands,
y'-gi-a ka-peicha ki to-cheil
You will be happy
ash-reicha
and it will be well with you.
v'-tov lach
Your wife shall be like a fruitful vine
esh-t'-cha k'-gefen po-ri-yah
Within your house, Your children
b'-yar-k'-tei vei-techa ba-neicha

(1) Zech 3:2 (2) Num 6:24-26 (3) Ps 121:4 (4) Gen 49:18

Prayer When Retiring at Night

בְּיַרְכְּתֵי בֵיתֶךָ בָּנֶיךָ like olive plants
kish-ti-lei zei-tim
כִּשְׁתִלֵי זֵיתִים around your table.
sa-viv l'-shul-cha-necha
סָבִיב לְשֻׁלְחָנֶךָ Behold, thus shall the man be blessed
hi-nei chi chen y'-vo-rach ga-ver
הִנֵּה כִי כֵן יְבֹרַךְ גָּבֶר who fears Adonai.
y'-rei Adonai
יְרֵא יהוה Adonai bless you from Zion,
y'-va-re-k'-cha Adonai mi-tzi-yon
יְבָרֶכְךָ יהוה מִצִּיּוֹן and may you see the prosperity
u-r'-ei b'-tuv
וּרְאֵה בְּטוּב of Jerusalem all the days of your life.
Y'-ru-sha-la-im kol y'-mei cha-yeicha
יְרוּשָׁלָיִם כֹּל יְמֵי חַיֶּיךָ Indeed, may you see
u-r'-ei
וּרְאֵה your children's children.
va-nim l'-va-neicha
בָנִים לְבָנֶיךָ Peace be upon Israel!
shalom al Yis-ra-el
שָׁלוֹם עַל יִשְׂרָאֵל

Tremble and do not sin.
rig-zu v'-al te-che-ta-u
רִגְזוּ וְאַל תֶּחֱטָאוּ Speak to your heart
im-ru vil-vav-chem
אִמְרוּ בִלְבַבְכֶם while upon your bed
al mish-kav-chem
עַל מִשְׁכַּבְכֶם and be silent. Selah.[1]
v'-do-mu selah
וְדֹמּוּ סֶלָה[1]

Lord of the world Who reigns supreme
adon o-lam asher ma-lach
אֲדוֹן עוֹלָם אֲשֶׁר מָלַךְ 'Ere all creation came to be
b'-terem kol y'-tzir niv-ra
בְּטֶרֶם כָּל יְצִיר נִבְרָא When by His will all things were wrought
l'-eit na-a-sah v'-chef-tzo kol
לְעֵת נַעֲשָׂה בְחֶפְצוֹ כֹּל The Name of our King was first made known.
a-zai melech sh'-mo nik-ra
אֲזַי מֶלֶךְ שְׁמוֹ נִקְרָא And when this age shall cease to be,
v'-a-cha-rei kich-lot ha-kol
וְאַחֲרֵי כִּכְלוֹת הַכֹּל He still shall reign in majesty
l'-va-do yim-loch no-ra

(1) Ps 4:5, cf. Eph 4:26

Prayer When Retiring at Night

לְבַדּוֹ יִמְלוֹךְ נוֹרָא	He was, He is,	
וְהוּא הָיָה וְהוּא הֹוֶה	and He will be	v'-hu ha-yah v'-hu ho-veh
וְהוּא יִהְיֶה	all glorious, eternally.	v'-hu yih-yeh
בְּתִפְאָרָה	Incomparable, the Lord is One;	b'-tif-a-rah
וְהוּא אֶחָד וְאֵין שֵׁנִי	No other can His nature share;	v'-hu e-chad v'-ein shei-ni
לְהַמְשִׁיל לוֹ לְהַחְבִּירָה	Without beginning, without end	l'-ham-shil lo l'-hach-bi-rah
בְּלִי רֵאשִׁית בְּלִי תַכְלִית	to Him all strength and majesty.	b'-li rei-shit b'-li tach-lit
וְלוֹ הָעוֹז וְהַמִּשְׂרָה	He is my living God Who saves	v'-lo ha-oz v'-ha-mis-rah
וְהוּא אֵלִי וְחַי גֹּאֲלִי	My rock when grief or sorrow falls	v'-hu ei-li v'-chai go-a-li
וְצוּר חֶבְלִי בְּעֵת צָרָה	My banner and my refuge strong,	v'-tzur chev-li b'-eit tza-rah
וְהוּא נִסִּי וּמָנוֹס לִי	My cup of life whenere' I call.	v'-hu ni-si u-ma-nos li
מְנָת כּוֹסִי בְּיוֹם אֶקְרָא	And in His hand I place my life,	m'-nat ko-si b'-yom ek-ra
בְּיָדוֹ אַפְקִיד רוּחִי	both when I sleep and when I wake.	b'-ya-do af-kid ru-chi
בְּעֵת אִישָׁן וְאָעִירָה	And with my soul and body too;	b'-eit i-shan v'-a-i-rah
וְעִם רוּחִי גְּוִיָּתִי	God is with me, there is no fear.[1]	v'-im ru-chi g'-vi-ya-ti
	Adonai li v'-lo i-ra	

Meditations from the Apostolic Scriptures
Philippians 4:8

סוֹף דָּבָר אַחַי	Finally, brethren,	sof davar a-chai
כָּל אֲשֶׁר אֱמֶת	whatever is true,	kol asher emet
כָּל מַה שֶׁנִּכְבָּד	whatever is honorable,	kol mah she-nich-bad
כָּל דָּבָר יָשָׁר טָהוֹר	whatever is right, is pure,	kol davar ya-shar ta-hor
מָלֵא נֹעַם	is lovely;	ma-leih no-am
כָּל אֲשֶׁר שִׁמְעוֹ טוֹב	whatever is of good repute,	kol asher shim-o tov

(1) *Adon Olam* is a free translation to make the English words singable.

Prayer When Retiring at Night

כָּל מַעֲשֶׂה נַעֲלֶה if there is any excellence,
kol ma-a-seh na-a-leh
וְכָל דָּבָר הָרָאוּי לְשֶׁבַח and if anything worthy of praise,
v'-kol davar ha-ra-u-i l'-she-vach
בְּאֵלֶּה יֶהְגֶּה לְבַבְכֶם meditate on these things.
b'-ei-leh yeh-geh l'-vav-chem

Matthew 5:3-10

אַשְׁרֵי עֲנִיֵּי הָרוּחַ Blessed are the poor in spirit,
ash-rei a-ni-yei ha-ru-ach
כִּי לָהֶם מַלְכוּת הַשָּׁמַיִם for theirs is the kingdom of heaven.
ki la-hem mal-chut ha-sha-ma-im
אַשְׁרֵי הָאֲבֵלִים Blessed are those who mourn,
ash-rei ha-a-vei-lim
כִּי הֵם יְנֻחָמוּ for they shall be comforted.
ki hem y'-nu-cha-mu
אַשְׁרֵי הָעֲנָוִים Blessed are the gentle,
ash-rei ha-a-no-vim
כִּי הֵם יִירְשׁוּ אֶת הָאָרֶץ for they shall inherit the earth.
ki hem yir-shu et ha-aretz
אַשְׁרֵי הָרְעֵבִים Blessed are those who hunger
ash-rei ha-r'-ei-vim
וְהַצְּמֵאִים לְצֶדֶק and thirst for righteousness,
v'-ha-tz'-mei-im l'-tzedek
כִּי הֵם יִשְׂבָּעוּ for they shall be satisfied.
ki hem yis-ba-u
אַשְׁרֵי הָרַחֲמָנִים Blessed are the merciful,
ash-rei ha-ra-cha-ma-nim
כִּי הֵם יְרֻחָמוּ for they shall receive mercy.
ki hem y'-ru-cha-mu
אַשְׁרֵי בָּרֵי לֵבָב Blessed are the pure in heart,
ash-rei ba-rei lei-vav
כִּי הֵם יִרְאוּ אֶת אֱלֹהִים for they shall see God.
ki hem yir-u et Elohim
אַשְׁרֵי רוֹדְפֵי שָׁלוֹם Blessed are the peacemakers,
ash-rei ro-d'-fei shalom
כִּי בְּנֵי אֱלֹהִים יִקָּרֵאוּ for they shall be called sons of God.
ki b'-nei Elohim yi-ka-rei-u
אַשְׁרֵי הַנִּרְדָּפִים Blessed are those who have been
ash-rei ha-nir-da-fim
בִּגְלַל הַצֶּדֶק persecuted for righteousness sake,
big-lal ha-tzedek
כִּי לָהֶם מַלְכוּת הַשָּׁמַיִם for theirs is the kingdom of heaven.
ki la-hem mal-chut ha-sha-ma-im

סדר ברית מילה Circumcision Service

When the child arrives in the room, all in attendance say:

בָּרוּךְ הַבָּא: **Blessed** is he who comes!
Baruch haba!

They place the baby upon the chair of Elijah, and the Mohel says:

זֶה הַכִּסֵּא שֶׁל אֵלִיָּהוּ — This is the seat of Elijah
ze ha-ki-sei shel E-li-ya-hu

הַנָּבִיא — the prophet,
ha-navi

זָכוּר לַטּוֹב — may he be remembered for good.
za-chur la-tov

לִישׁוּעָתְךָ קִוִּיתִי יהוה: — For Your salvation I have hoped, Adonai.
li-shu-a-t'-cha ki-vi-ti Adonai

שִׂבַּרְתִּי לִישׁוּעָתְךָ יהוה — I have longed for Your salvation, Adonai,
si-bar-ti li-shu-a-t'-cha Adonai

וּמִצְוֹתֶיךָ עָשִׂיתִי:[1] — And Your statutes I have done.[1]
u-mitz-vo-techa a-si-ti

אֵלִיָּהוּ מַלְאַךְ הַבְּרִית — Elijah, messenger of the covenant,
E-li-ya-hu mal-ach ha-b'-rit

הִנֵּה שֶׁלְּךָ לְפָנֶיךָ — Behold, yours is before you—
hi-nei she-l'-cha l'-fa-necha

עֲמוֹד עַל יְמִינִי וְסָמְכֵנִי — stand at my right hand and support me.
a-mod al y'-mi-ni v'-sam-kei-ni

שִׂבַּרְתִּי לִישׁוּעָתְךָ יהוה — I have longed for Your salvation, Adonai.
si-barti li-shu-a-t'-cha Adonai

שָׂשׂ אָנֹכִי עַל אִמְרָתֶךָ — I rejoice upon Your word
sos a-no-chi al im-ra-techa

כְּמוֹצֵא שָׁלָל רָב:[2] — like one who finds much fortune.[2]
k'-mo-tzei sha-lal rav

שָׁלוֹם רָב לְאֹהֲבֵי — Great is the peace of those who love
shalom rav l'-o-ha-vei

תוֹרָתֶךָ וְאֵין לָמוֹ — Your Torah, and to them there is no
tora-techa v'-ein la-mo

מִכְשׁוֹל:[3] — stumbling.[3]
mich-shol

אַשְׁרֵי תִּבְחַר — Blessed is he whom You choose
ash-rei tiv-char

וּתְקָרֵב — and draw near
u-t'-ka-reiv

יִשְׁכֹּן חֲצֵרֶיךָ:[4] — that he might dwell in Your courts.[4]
yish-kon cha-tzei-recha

(1) Ps 119:166 (2) Ps 119:162 (3) Ps 119:165 (4) Ps 65:4

Circumcision Service

All present respond:

נִשְׂבְּעָה **May** we be satisfied
Nis-b'-ah
בְּטוּב בֵּיתֶךָ with the goodness of Your house,
b'-tuv bei-techa
קְדֹשׁ הֵיכָלֶךָ: the holiness of Your sanctuary.
k'-dosh hei-cha-lecha

They place the baby in the hands of the Sandak and the Mohel pronounces the blessings:

ברכות המילה **Blessings of the Circumcision**

בָּרוּךְ אַתָּה יהוה Blessed are You, Adonai our God
Baruch ata Adonai,
אֱלֹהֵינוּ מֶלֶךְ הָעוֹלָם King of the universe, Who
Eloheinu melech ha-olam
אֲשֶׁר קִדְּשָׁנוּ בְּמִצְוֹתָיו sanctified us with His commandments
asher ki-d'-shanu b'-mitz-vo-tav
וְצִוָּנוּ עַל הַמִּילָה: and commanded us about circumcision.
v'-tzi-va-nu al ha-milah

During the circumcison, the child's father says the following blessings:

בָּרוּךְ אַתָּה יהוה אֱלֹהֵינוּ Blessed are You, Adonai our God
Baruch ata Adonai, Eloheinu
מֶלֶךְ הָעוֹלָם אֲשֶׁר King of the universe, Who
melech ha-olam asher
קִדְּשָׁנוּ בְּמִצְוֹתָיו sanctified us with His commandments,
ki-d'-shanu b'-mitz-vo-tav
וְצִוָּנוּ לְהַכְנִיסוֹ and commanded us to bring him into
v'-tzi-va-nu l'-hach-ni-so
בִּבְרִיתוֹ שֶׁל אַבְרָהָם the covenant of Abraham
biv-ri-to shel Av-ra-ham
אָבִינוּ our father.
a-vinu.

All in attendance say:

אָמֵן כְּשֵׁם שֶׁנִּכְנַס **Amen.** Just as he has entered
Amein. K'-shem she-nich-nas
לַבְּרִית into the covenant,
la-b'-rit
כֵּן יִכָּנֵס so may he be gathered
ken yi-ka-neis

Circumcision Service

לְתוֹרָה וּלְהַאֲמִין	to the Torah, to faith	l'-tora u-l'-ha-a-min
בְּיֵשׁוּעַ הַמָּשִׁיחַ	in Yeshua the Messiah,	b'-Yeshua HaMashiach
וּלְחֻפָּה	to the Chuppah,	u-l'-chu-pah
וּלְמַעֲשִׂים טוֹבִים	and to good deeds.	u-l'-ma-a-sim to-vim

After the Mohel is finished, the blessing over the wine is said

בָּרוּךְ אַתָּה יהוה	**Blessed** are You, Adonai our God	Baruch ata Adonai
אֱלֹהֵינוּ מֶלֶךְ הָעוֹלָם	King of the universe, Creator of	Eloheinu melech ha-o-lam
בּוֹרֵא פְּרִי הַגָּפֶן	the fruit of the vine.	bo-rei p'-ri ha-gafen

The Mohel continues with the blessings:

בָּרוּךְ אַתָּה יהוה אֱלֹהֵינוּ	Blessed are You, Adonai our God	Baruch ata Adonai Eloheinu
מֶלֶךְ הָעוֹלָם אֲשֶׁר קִדַּשׁ	King of the universe, Who sanctified	melech ha-olam asher ki-dash
יְדִיד מִבֶּטֶן	the beloved one from the womb	y'-did mi-beten
וְחֹק בִּשְׁאֵרוֹ שָׂם	and a statute He set in his flesh,	v'-chok bish-ei-ro sam
וְצֶאֱצָאָיו חָתַם	and sealed his offspring	v'-tze-e-tza-av chatam
בְּאוֹת בְּרִית קֹדֶשׁ	with the sign of the holy covenant.	b'-ot b'-rit kodesh
עַל כֵּן בִּשְׂכַר זֹאת	Therefore on account of this,	al ken bis-char zot
אֵל חַי חֶלְקֵנוּ צוּרֵנוּ	living God, our Portion, our Rock,	el chai chel-keinu tzu-reinu
צַוֵּה לְהַצִּיל יְדִידוּת	command to rescue the beloved of	tza-vei l'-ha-tzil y'-di-dut
שְׁאֵרֵנוּ מִשַּׁחַת	our remnant from destruction	sh'-ei-reinu mi-sha-chat
לְמַעַן בְּרִיתוֹ אֲשֶׁר	because of His covenant which	l'-ma-an b'-ri-to asher
שָׂם בִּבְשָׂרֵנוּ	He placed in our flesh.	sam biv-sar-einu

Circumcision Service

בָּרוּךְ אַתָּה יהוה
כּוֹרֵת הַבְּרִית
Blessed are You, Adonai,
Baruch ata Adonai
Maker of the covenant.
ko-reit ha-b'-rit

אֱלֹהֵינוּ וֵאלֹהֵי אֲבוֹתֵינוּ
קַיֵּם אֶת הַיֶּלֶד הַזֶּה
לְאָבִיו וּלְאִמּוֹ
וְיִקָּרֵא שְׁמוֹ בְּיִשְׂרָאֵל
(_____ בֶּן _____)
יִשְׂמַח הָאָב בְּיוֹצֵא
חֲלָצָיו וְתָגֵל אִמּוֹ
בִּפְרִי בִטְנָהּ כַּכָּתוּב:
יִשְׂמַח אָבִיךָ וְאִמֶּךָ
וְתָגֵל יוֹלַדְתֶּךָ:
וְנֶאֱמַר וָאֶעֱבֹר עָלַיִךְ
וָאֶרְאֵךְ מִתְבּוֹסֶסֶת
בְּדָמָיִךְ וָאֹמַר לָךְ
בְּדָמַיִךְ חֲיִי וָאֹמַר לָךְ
בְּדָמַיִךְ חֲיִי: וְנֶאֱמַר
זָכַר לְעוֹלָם בְּרִיתוֹ
דָּבָר צִוָּה
לְאֶלֶף דּוֹר: אֲשֶׁר
כָּרַת אֶת אַבְרָהָם

Our God and God of our fathers,
Eloheinu vei-lo-hei a-vo-teinu
establish this child
ka-yeim et ha-yeled ha-ze
to his father and mother,
l'-a-viv u-l'-imo
and his name shall be called in Israel:
v'-yi-ka-rei sh'-mo b'-Yis-ra-el
_____ son of _____
ben
May his father rejoice in his
yis-mach ha-av b'-yo-tzei
offspring, and his mother be glad
cha-la-tzav v'-ta-geil imo
in the fruit of her womb, as it written:
bif-ri bit-na kakatuv
"Let your father and mother rejoice
Yis-mach avi-cha v'-i-mecha.
and she who birthed you exalt."[1]
v'-ta-geil yo-lad-techa
And it is said, "And I passed over you
v'ne-e-mar va-e-e-vor a-la-yich
and I saw you staggering
va-er-eich mit-bo-seset
in your blood and I said to you,
b'-da-ma-yich va-omar lach
"in your blood—live!" And I said to you,
b'damayich chayi va-omar lach
"in your blood—live!"[2] And it is said,
b'-da-ma-yich cha-yi v'ne-e-mar
"He remembered forever His covenant,
zachar l'-olam b'-ri-to
the word He commanded to
davar tziva
a thousand generations, which He
l'-elef dod asher
enacted (as a covenant) with Abraham
karat et Avraham

(1) Prov 23:25 (2) Ezek 16:6

Circumcision Service

וּשְׁבוּעָתוֹ לְיִצְחָק:	and His oath to Isaac.
	u-sh'-vu-ato l'-yitz-chak
וַיַּעֲמִידֶהָ לְיַעֲקֹב לְחֹק	And established it for Jacob for a statute,
	va-ya-a-mi-deha l'-Ya-a-cov l'-chok
לְיִשְׂרָאֵל בְּרִית עוֹלָם[1]	to Israel, an eternal covenant."[1]
	l'-Yis-ra-el b'-rit olam
וְנֶאֱמַר: וַיָּמָל אַבְרָהָם	And it is said, "Abraham circumcised
	v'-ne-e-mar: va-ya-mal Avraham
אֶת יִצְחָק בְּנוֹ	Isaac his son
	et Yitz-chak b'-no
בֶּן שְׁמוֹנַת יָמִים	when he was eight days old
	ben sh'-mo-nat yamim
כַּאֲשֶׁר צִוָּה אֹתוֹ אֱלֹהִים[2]	just as God had commanded him."[2]
	ka-asher tzi-va oto Elohim
הוֹדוּ לַיהוה כִּי טוֹב	Give thanks to Adonai for He is good
	Ho-du la-donai ki tov
כִּי לְעוֹלָם חַסְדּוֹ:[3]	For His kindness is forever.[3]
	ki l'olam chasdo.

Those in attendance respond:

הוֹדוּ לַיהוה כִּי טוֹב	**Give thanks** to Adonai for He is good,
	Hodu la-donai ki tov
כִּי לְעוֹלָם חַסְדּוֹ:	For His kindness is forever.
	ki l'olam chasdo
_____ בֶּן _____	_____ son of _____
	ben
זֶה הַקָּטֹן	this little one,
	ze ha-ka-ton
גָּדוֹל יִהְיֶה כְּשֵׁם	May he become great. Even as
	ga-dol yih-yeh k'-shem
שֶׁנִּכְנַס לַבְּרִית	he was gathered to the covenant,
	she-nich-nas la-b'-rit
כֵּן יִכָּנֵס לְתוֹרָה	so may he be gathered to the Torah
	ken yi-ka-nes l'-torah
וּלְהַאֲמִין בְּיֵשׁוּעַ הַמָּשִׁיחַ	and to faith in Yeshua the Messiah,
	u-l'-ha-a-min b'Yeshua HaMashiach
וּלְחֻפָּה	to the chuppah
	u-l'-chuppah
וּלְמַעֲשִׂים טוֹבִים. אָמֵן:	and to good deeds. Amen.
	u-l'-ma-a-sim tovim. Amein.

(1) Ps 105:8-10 (2) Gen 17:23 (3) Ps 136

Marriage Service

ברכות אירוסין ונשואין Marriage Service

The following blessings are said under the marriage chuppah:

בָּרוּךְ אַתָּה יהוה אֱלֹהֵינוּ Blessed are You, Adonai our God
baruch ata Adonai Eloheinu
מֶלֶךְ הָעוֹלָם King of the Universe
melech ha-olam
בּוֹרֵא פְּרִי הַגָּפֶן: Creator of the fruit of the vine
bo-rei p'-ri ha-ga-fen

בָּרוּךְ אַתָּה יהוה אֱלֹהֵינוּ Blessed are You, Adonai our God
baruch ata Adonai Eloheinu
מֶלֶךְ הָעוֹלָם King of the Universe,
melech ha-o-lam
אֲשֶׁר קִדְּשָׁנוּ Who sanctified us
asher ki-d'-sha-nu
בְּמִצְוֹתָיו with His commandments
b'-mitz-vo-taiv
וְצִוָּנוּ and commanded us
v'-tzi-vanu
עַל הָעֲרָיוֹת regarding forbidden relationships
al ha-a-rai-ot
וְאָסַר לָנוּ and forbade us
v'-a-sar lanu
אֶת הָאֲרוּסוֹת betrothed women
et ha-a-ru-sot
וְהִתִּיר לָנוּ and permitted us
v'-hi-tir lanu
אֶת הַנְּשׂוּאוֹת לָנוּ those rightly married to us
et ha-n'-su-ot lanu
עַל יְדֵי חֻפָּה by means of the *chuppah*
al y'-dei chuppah
וְקִדּוּשִׁין and consecration.
v'-ki-du-shin
בָּרוּךְ אַתָּה יהוה Blessed are You, Adonai,
baruch ata Adonai
מְקַדֵּשׁ עַמּוֹ יִשְׂרָאֵל Who sanctified His people Israel
m'-ka-deish amo Yis-ra-el
עַל יְדֵי חֻפָּה by means of the *chuppah*
al y'-dei chuppah
וְקִדּוּשִׁין and consecration.
v'-ki-du-shin

Marriage Service

The groom and bride drink from the cup, and then the groom consecrates his bride to him with a ring, in the presence of appropriate witnesses:

הֲרֵי אַתְּ מְקֻדֶּשֶׁת לִי You are hereby consecrated to me
ha-rei at m'-ku-deshet li
בְּטַבַּעַת זוּ with this ring
b'-ta-ba-at zu
כְּדַת מֹשֶׁה according to the law of Moses
k'-dat Mo-sheh
וְיִשְׂרָאֵל and Israel.
v'-Yis-ra-el

The marriage contract (ketuvah) is read and presented to the bride. A second cup of wine is poured and following blessings recited:

שבע ברכות **The Seven Blessings**

בָּרוּךְ אַתָּה יהוה אֱלֹהֵינוּ 1. Blessed are You, Adonai our God,
baruch ata Adonai Eloheinu
מֶלֶךְ הָעוֹלָם King of the Universe
melech ha-olam
בּוֹרֵא פְּרִי הַגָּפֶן Creator of the fruit of the vine.
bo-rei p'-ri ha-gafen

בָּרוּךְ אַתָּה יהוה אֱלֹהֵינוּ 2. Blessed are You, Adonai our God,
baruch ata Adonai Eloheinu
מֶלֶךְ הָעוֹלָם King of the Universe
melech ha-o-lam
שֶׁהַכֹּל בָּרָא Who created everything
she-ha-kol ba-ra
לִכְבוֹדוֹ for His glory.
lich-vo-do

בָּרוּךְ אַתָּה יהוה אֱלֹהֵינוּ 3. Blessed are You Adonai our God,
baruch ata Adonai Eloheinu
מֶלֶךְ הָעוֹלָם King of the Univese,
melech ha-o-lam
יוֹצֵר הָאָדָם Who formed mankind.
yo-tzeir ha-a-dam

Marriage Service

4. Blessed are You, Adonai our God, בָּרוּךְ אַתָּה יהוה אֱלֹהֵינוּ
baruch ata Adonai Eloheinu
King of Universe, מֶלֶךְ הָעוֹלָם
melech ha-o-lam
Who formed mankind אֲשֶׁר יָצַר אֶת הָאָדָם
asher ya-tzar et ha-a-dam
in His image, בְּצַלְמוֹ
b'-tzal-mo
in the image of His likeness; בְּצֶלֶם דְּמוּת תַּבְנִיתוֹ
b'-tzelem d'-mut tav-ni-to
and formed for him, וְהִתְקִין לוֹ
v'-hit-kin lo
from his own self, מִמֶּנּוּ
mi-menu
a wife forever. בִּנְיַן עֲדֵי עַד
bin-yan a-dei ad
Blessed are You, Adonai, בָּרוּךְ אַתָּה יהוה
baruch ata Adonai
Former of mankind. יוֹצֵר הָאָדָם
yo-tzeir ha-a-dam

5. May the barren one[1] rejoice and exalt שׂוֹשׂ תָּשִׂישׂ וְתָגֵל הָעֲקָרָה
sos ta-sis v'-ta-geil ha-a-ka-rah
in the gathering of her children בְּקִבּוּץ בָּנֶיהָ
b'-ki-butz ba-neiha
to her midst with joy. לְתוֹכָהּ בְּשִׂמְחָה
l'-to-chah b'-sim-chah
Blessed are You, Adonai, בָּרוּךְ אַתָּה יהוה
baruch ata Adonai
Who causes Zion to rejoice מְשַׂמֵּחַ צִיּוֹן
m'-sa-meich Tzi-yon
with her children. בְּבָנֶיהָ
b'-va-nei-ha

6. Give abundant joy שַׂמֵּחַ תְּשַׂמַּח
sa-mei-ach t'-sa-mach
to these beloved companions רֵעִים הָאֲהוּבִים
rei-im ha-a-hu-vim
as You gave joy to Your creation כְּשַׂמֵּחֲךָ יְצִירְךָ
k'-sa-mei-cha-cha y'-tzir-cha
in the Garden of Eden of old. בְּגַן עֵדֶן מִקֶּדֶם
b'-gan ei-den mi-kedem
Blessed are You, Adonai, בָּרוּךְ אַתָּה יהוה
baruch ata Adonai

(1) the barren one refers to Jerusalem

מְשַׂמֵּחַ	Who gives rejoicing to	
	m'-sh-mei-ach	
חָתָן וְכַלָּה	the groom and the bride.	
	cha-tan v'-cha-lah	
בָּרוּךְ אַתָּה יהוה אֱלֹהֵינוּ	7. Blessed are You, Adonai our God,	
	baruch ata Adonai Eloheinu	
מֶלֶךְ הָעוֹלָם	King of the Universe,	
	melech ha-o-lam	
אֲשֶׁר בָּרָא שָׂשׂוֹן וְשִׂמְחָה	Who created joy and rejoicing,	
	asher ba-ra sa-son v'-sim-chah	
חָתָן וְכַלָּה גִּילָה רִנָּה	groom and bride, exultation and song,	
	cha-tan v'-cha-lah gi-lah ri-nah	
דִּיצָה וְחֶדְוָה	pleasure and delight,	
	di-tzah v'-che-d'-vah	
אַהֲבָה וְאַחֲוָה	love and companionship,	
	a-ha-vah v'-a-cha-vah	
וְשָׁלוֹם וְרֵעוּת	peace and friendship.	
	v'-shalom v'-rei-ut	
מְהֵרָה יהוה אֱלֹהֵינוּ	Soon, Adonai our God,	
	m'-hei-rah Adonai Eloheinu	
יִשָּׁמַע בְּעָרֵי יְהוּדָה	may there be heard in the cities of Judah	
	yi-sha-ma b'-a-rei Y'-hu-dah	
וּבְחֻצוֹת יְרוּשָׁלַיִם	and in the streets of Jerusalem	
	u-v'-chu-tzot Y'-ru-sha-laim	
קוֹל שָׂשׂוֹן וְקוֹל שִׂמְחָה	the sound of joy and rejoicing,	
	kol sa-son v'-kol sim-chah	
קוֹל חָתָן וְקוֹל כַּלָּה[1]	the voice of the groom and bride,[1]	
	kol cha-tan v'-kol ka-lah	
קוֹל מִצְהֲלוֹת חֲתָנִים	the sound of grooms' jubilation	
	kol mitz-ha-lot cha-ta-nim	
מֵחֻפָּתָם	from their *chuppah*,	
	mei-chu-pa-tam	
וּנְעָרִים	and of young men	
	u-n'-a-rim	
מִמִּשְׁתֵּה נְגִינָתָם	from their feasts of song!	
	mi-mish-teih n'-gi-na-tam	
בָּרוּךְ אַתָּה יהוה	Blessed are You, Adonai,	
	baruch ata Adonai	
מְשַׂמֵּחַ חָתָן	Who causes the groom to rejoice	
	m'-sa-mei-ach cha-tan	
עִם הַכַּלָּה	with the bride.	
	im ha-ka-lah	

(1) Jer 33:10-11

Prayers and Blessings
תפילה וברכות

Prayer for Travlers

יְהִי רָצוֹן מִלְּפָנֶיךָ יהוה	May it be your will, Adonai	y'-hi ratzon mi-l'-fa-neicha Adonai
אֱלֹהֵינוּ וֵאלֹהֵי אֲבוֹתֵינוּ	our God, and God of our fathers,	Eloheinu vei-lohei a-vo-teinu
שֶׁתּוֹלִיכֵנוּ לְשָׁלוֹם	that You lead us to peace,	she-to-li-cheinu l'-shalom
וְתַצְעִידֵנוּ לְשָׁלוֹם	guide our footsteps to peace,	v'-tatz-i-deinu l'-shalom
וְתַדְרִיכֵנוּ לְשָׁלוֹם	make our way toward peace,	v'-tad-ri-cheinu l'-shalom
וְתַגִּיעֵנוּ לִמְחוֹז חֶפְצֵנוּ	and bring us to our desired destination	v'-ta-gi-einu lim-choz chef-tzeinu
לְחַיִּים וּלְשִׂמְחָה וּלְשָׁלוֹם	for life, happiness, and peace.	l'-cha-yim u-l'-sim-cha u-l'-shalom
וְתַצִּילֵנוּ מִכַּף	May You rescue us from the hand	v'-ta-tzi-leinu mi-kaf
כָּל אוֹיֵב וְאוֹרֵב בַּדֶּרֶךְ	of every enemy or ambush on the way,	kol o-yeiv v'-o-reiv ba-derech
וּמִכָּל מִינֵי פֻּרְעָנִיּוֹת	and from all kinds of trouble	u-mi-kol mi-nei fur-o-ni-ot
הַמִּתְרַגְּשׁוֹת לָבוֹא לָעוֹלָם	that happen in this world.	ha-mit-ra-g'-shot la-vo la-o-lam
וְתִשְׁלַח בְּרָכָה בְּכָל	Send blessing upon all	v'-tish-lach b'-ra-chah b'-kol
מַעֲשֵׂה יָדֵינוּ	the work of our hands	ma-a-seih ya-deinu
וְתִתְּנֵנוּ לְחֵן וּלְחֶסֶד	and grant us grace, lovingkindness,	v'-ti-t'-neinu l'-chen u-l'-chesed
וּלְרַחֲמִים בְּעֵינֶיךָ	and mercy in Your eyes	u-l'-ra-cha-mim b'-ei-neicha
וּבְעֵינֵי כָל רוֹאֵינוּ	and in the eyes of all who see us.	u-v'-ei-nei chol ro-einu
וְתִשְׁמַע קוֹל תַּחֲנוּנֵינוּ	Hear the voice of our supplication,	v'-rish-ma kol ta-cha-nu-neinu
כִּי אֵל שׁוֹמֵעַ	for You are the Almighty Who hears	ki El sho-mei-a
תְּפִלָּה וְתַחֲנוּן אָתָּה	prayer and supplication.	t'-fi-la v'-ta-cha-nun ata
בָּרוּךְ אַתָּה יהוה	Blessed are You, Adonai,	baruch ata Adonai
שׁוֹמֵעַ תְּפִלָּה	Who hears prayer.	sho-mei-a t'-fi-lah

Some also recite the following Scriptures: Gen 32:2-3; 49:18; Ex 23:20; Ps 29:11

Prayers and Blessings

Blessing for eating grains

בָּרוּךְ אַתָּה יהוה אֱלֹהֵינוּ Blessed are You, Adonai our God,
    baruch ata Adonai Eloheinu
מֶלֶךְ הָעוֹלָם King of the Universe,
    melech ha-o-lam
בּוֹרֵא מִינֵי מְזוֹנוֹת: Creator of all kinds of nourishment.
    bo-rei mi-nei m'-zo-rot

Blessing for eating fruit from trees:

בָּרוּךְ אַתָּה יהוה אֱלֹהֵינוּ Blessed are You, Adonai our God,
    baruch ata Adonai Eloheinu
מֶלֶךְ הָעוֹלָם King of the Universe,
    melech ha-o-lam
בּוֹרֵא פְּרִי הָעֵץ: Creator of the fruit of the tree.
    bo-rei p'-ri ha-eitz

Blessing for eating vegetables grown from the ground:

בָּרוּךְ אַתָּה יהוה אֱלֹהֵינוּ Blessed are You, Adonai our God,
    baruch ata Adonai Eloheinu
מֶלֶךְ הָעוֹלָם King of the Universe,
    melech ha-o-lam
בּוֹרֵא פְּרִי הָאֲדָמָה: Creator of the fruit of the ground.
    bo-rei p'-ri ha-a-da-mah

Blessing for eating meat, fish, milk, eggs, cheese, mushrooms, and before drinking all liquids except wine and grape juice:

בָּרוּךְ אַתָּה יהוה אֱלֹהֵינוּ Blessed are You, Adonai our God,
    baruch ata Adonai Eloheinu
מֶלֶךְ הָעוֹלָם King of the Universe,
    melech ha-o-lam
שֶׁהַכֹּל נִהְיֶה בִּדְבָרוֹ: by Whose word all things exist.
    she-ha-kol nih-yeh bid-va-ro

Blessing when witnessing phenomenal sights:

בָּרוּךְ אַתָּה יהוה אֱלֹהֵינוּ Blessed are You, Adonai our God,
    baruch ata Adonai Eloheinu
מֶלֶךְ הָעוֹלָם King of the Universe,
    melech ha-o-lam
עוֹשֶׂה מַעֲשֵׂה בְרֵאשִׁית: Who makes the work of creation.
    o-seih ma-a-seih v'-rei-shit

Prayers and Blessings

Blessing when seeing a rainbow:

בָּרוּךְ אַתָּה יהוה אֱלֹהֵינוּ
Blessed are You, Adonai our God,
baruch ata Adonai Eloheinu

מֶלֶךְ הָעוֹלָם
King of the Universe,
melech ha-o-lam

זוֹכֵר הַבְּרִית
Who remembers the covenant
zo-cheir ha-b'-rit

וְנֶאֱמָן בִּבְרִיתוֹ
and is faithful to His covenant
v'-ne-e-man biv-ri-to

וְקַיָּם בְּמַאֲמָרוֹ:
and fulfills His word.
v'-ka-yam b'-ma-a-maro

Blessing for attaching a Mezuzah:

בָּרוּךְ אַתָּה יהוה אֱלֹהֵינוּ
Blessed are You, Adonai our God,
baruch ata Adonai Eloheinu

מֶלֶךְ הָעוֹלָם
King of the Universe,
melech ha-o-lam

אֲשֶׁר קִדְּשָׁנוּ
Who sanctified us with His
asher ki-d'-shanu

בְּמִצְוֹתָיו
commandments,
b'-mitz-vo-taiv

וְצִוָּנוּ לִקְבּוֹעַ מְזוּזָה:
and commanded us to attach a mezuzah.
v'-tzi-vanu lik-bo-a m'-zu-zah

Blessing when separating challah:

בָּרוּךְ אַתָּה יהוה אֱלֹהֵינוּ
Blessed are You, Adonai our God,
baruch ata Adonai Eloheinu

מֶלֶךְ הָעוֹלָם
King of the Universe,
melech ha-o-lam

אֲשֶׁר קִדְּשָׁנוּ
Who sanctified us with His
asher ki-d'-shanu

בְּמִצְוֹתָיו
commandments,
b'-mitz-vo-taiv

וְצִוָּנוּ
and commanded us
v'-tzi-vanu

לְהַפְרִישׁ חַלָּה
to separate challah
l'-haf-rish cha-lah

מִן הָעִסָּה:[1]
from the dough.[1]
min ha-i-sah

---

(1) cf. Num 15:20